James Orchard Halliwell-Phillipps

A Calendar of the Shakespearean Rarities

Drawings and Engravings Preserved at Hollingbury Copse, near Brighton

James Orchard Halliwell-Phillipps

A Calendar of the Shakespearean Rarities
Drawings and Engravings Preserved at Hollingbury Copse, near Brighton

ISBN/EAN: 9783337151409

Printed in Europe, USA, Canada, Australia, Japan

Cover: Foto ©Thomas Meinert / pixelio.de

More available books at **www.hansebooks.com**

A CALENDAR

OF THE

SHAKESPEAREAN RARITIES,

DRAWINGS AND ENGRAVINGS,

PRESERVED AT

HOLLINGBURY COPSE, NEAR BRIGHTON,

that quaint wigwam on the Sussex Downs which has the honour of sheltering more record and artistic evidences connected with the personal history of the Great Dramatist than are to be found in any other of the World's libraries.

"But now he's gone, and my idolatrous fancy
Must sanctify his relics."

London :
For Special Circulation and for Presents only.

MDCCCLXXXVII.

PREFACE.

For nearly half a century I have been an ardent Shakespearean collector, being most likely the only survivor of the little band who attended the sale of the library of George Chalmers somewhere about the year 1840. But for a long time, attempting too much in several directions with insufficient means, and harassed, moreover, by a succession of lawsuits, including two in the Court of Torture,—I mean Chancery,—I was unable to retain my accumulations: and thus it came to pass that book-case full after bookcase full were disposed of, some by private contract, many under the vibrations of the auctioneer's hammer. This state of affairs continued till February, 1872, but since that period, by a strict limitation of my competitive resources to one subject,—the Life of Shakespeare,—I have managed to jog along without parting with a single article of any description, nor is there a probability that the collection described in the following pages will ever be dispersed.

When the reader, or, rather, I should say, the inspector of this calendar bears in mind that, exclusive of the Blight sketches, all but the whole of this collection has been formed within the last fifteen years, and that it already stands pre-eminent amidst the libraries of the world in no less than four of the most important divisions of Shakespeareana, the product will be regarded with no small astonishment by those who know how exceedingly difficult it is, and how very rarely as a rule it is possible, to obtain even a single document of the sixteenth or seventeeth century, or a single original drawing of the eighteenth, that is perceptibly illustrative of the poet's biography. Half-a-dozen of either would be infinitely more difficult to obtain than an impenetrable fifty-thousand-volume library of modern books on the works of the great dramatist. The four divisions to which allusion has here been made are,—1. Early engraved portraits of Shakespeare.—2. Authentic personal relics.—3. Documentary evidences respecting his estates and individuals who are connected with his biography.—4. Artistic illustrations of localities connected with his personal history.

1. The most important of these is of course the copy of the Droeshout portrait (No. 220) of Shakespeare *in its original proof state before it was altered by an inferior hand into the vitiated form in which it has been so long familiar to the public.* This is the earliest engraved portrait of the great dramatist, and differs so materially from the later impressions that it gives a new and more pleasing idea of his features. Here we have the most reliable likeness of Shakespeare in existence, the only one which has not been injuriously tampered with, while, at the same time, the evidences of its genuineness and its antiquity are incontestable, and it is most unfortunate that the appliances of modern art are inadequate to its satisfactory reproduction. The collection includes several other impressions of the engraving in various states of the plate, as well as all the known engraved portraits of the great dramatist up to

that which was published by Rowe in 1709; but scarcely any have been admitted that were issued after that year, none of the latter being of real value, and very few that can be fairly said to be of the slightest interest.

2. Very few authentic personal relics of the great dramatist, that is to say, articles that were at one time *indubitably* in his own possession, are known to be in existence. They are, in fact, restricted to the will, now preserved at Somerset House, and to a small number of title-deeds, for there is not a single other domestic memorial of any description the genuineness of which is not open to either doubt or suspicion. But that the title-deeds of his unmortgaged estates, those that are dated previously to the twenty-third of April, 1616, were once in his own hands, does not admit of rational question; documents of this kind having been, in his day, jealously guarded by their owners, never being entrusted, as now, to the custody of solicitors. Of these title-deeds there are no fewer than six in the present collection, the four New Place indentures, Nos. 143 to 146, and the two (No. 140) original indentures of a fine between the poet and Hercules Underhill that was levied in the year 1602.

To these may in all probability, though not with absolute certainty, be added the original conveyance (No. 148) of Shakespeare's Blackfriars estate, 1613, which was unquestionably on the table when the poet executed the concurrent mortgage, and as it must have been formally passed over to him, it is altogether most unlikely that he did not touch it with his own hands. This was the deed that was enrolled in Chancery soon after the purchase, the official endorsement still remaining in a perfect state of preservation, and it was for many years one of the leading treasures of the Sainsbury collection. It subsequently passed into that of the late Sir William Tite, who very kindly, on December the 20th, 1872, transferred the purchase to me. I afterwards had the good fortune to acquire the other Shakespearean ornament of the Sainsbury hoard, the original deed (No. 149) transferring the house in the Blackfriars in trust to follow the directions of the poet's will, a document that was executed in 1618, and handed over to his daughter Susannah. A record of later date respecting the same estate, the exemplification of a fine that was levied in 1647, will be observed at No. 124.

3. Amongst these may be noticed, in addition to the six interesting title-deeds above-mentioned respecting New Place, the series of documents relating to the same estate, Nos. 125 to 131; two deeds (Nos. 133, 258) each having the autograph of the poet's Sir Thomas Lucy, the first with a perfect impression of the seal exhibiting the three luces; the deed (No. 142) of 1596, witnessed by John Shakespeare; a large number of records of Hathaway families, including several relating to a house at Stratford that undoubtedly belonged to relatives of the poet's Anne, two of them mentioning the boundary of his estate; the Clopton cartulary (No. 1) in which is found the earliest discovered notice of any part of Shakespeare's property; other documents with the very rare signatures of John a' Combe; Thomas Greene, the poet's cousin; Walter Roche, his schoolmaster; Francis Collins, his solicitor; Thomas Combe, to whom he left his sword; and Shakespeare Hart. There are also two with the autographs of the Earls of Southampton and Essex.

4. It is very difficult to meet with pictorial illustrations of the Life of Shakespeare that belong to even a small antiquity. With the exception of the very few engravings to be met with in periodicals, in editions of the poet's works, and in Ireland's Warwickshire Avon, and which are sufficiently common, any of the kind which were executed before the commencement of the present century are of exceedingly rare occurrence. The Bodleian Library, so rich in English topography, has none; while in that enormous literary warehouse, the British Museum, there are hardly any of the slightest interest. There are, indeed, only two large and important collections of drawings and engravings illustrative of Shakespearean biography. One of these, that now preserved at the Birth-Place, was formed by the late Mr. W. O. Hunt and myself in years gone by, when we ransacked Stratford-on-Avon and its neighbourhood for every relic of the kind. The other, the present one, is all but entirely the result of purchases from other localities. Each collection is, at present, of unique interest, and is likely to remain so. It is not probable that another, of equal value to either, could now be formed, and even many of the engravings and lithographs of forty or fifty years of age are of great rarity, obtainable only by accident.

The biographical student should guard against the too easy rejection of comparatively modern illustrations. Every representation of an old building, however recent, if taken from nature and before its alteration, is of a definite and permanent value. Thus, for example, the only perfect evidences of the state of the back of the Birth-Place previously to its restoration were preserved in a number of photographic plates executed in 1854, now in the museum of that institution, but so faded that they are all but valueless; and had I not had the precaution of having had copies made of them before many of the details had disappeared, those evidences would have been lost for ever. The copies are in the unrivalled series of Birth-Place illustrations calendared in the following pages. No early views of the abovementioned portions of the building have yet been discovered, and even late unpublished sketches of the street-exterior are of such immense rarity that I thought myself fortunate in obtaining Shepherd's water-colour view (No. 668) taken about the year 1830, and Neale's large pencil sketch (No. 733) taken in July, 1820. As for original drawings of the last century, many readers will be surprised to hear that only three are known to exist, the so-called one in the British Museum being a mere variation of the published engraving of 1769. Two of those three are in the present collection, Greene's sketch, No. 654, and Ireland's view taken in 1792, No. 733. Some years ago there was a fourth, a large sketch by Jordan, but it perished with the rest of the Staunton library in 1879. A facsimile tracing, in the volume described at No. 733, is now its unique representative.

The collection of printed Shakespeareana has been mainly restricted to books that were issued before the Restoration of Charles the Second in 1660, the few belonging to a later period owing their admission to their being in some way either illustrative of the poet's biography, or of practices in the representation of his dramas that may have been adopted from those that had been current at the Globe or Blackfriars. Amongst the articles in this division may be mentioned the all but unique surreptitious edition of Pierce Penilesse, 1592, in which there is the earliest allusion to any of the works of Shakespeare that has yet been discovered; the drama of Promos and Cassandra, the foundation-play of Measure for Measure, 1578; the Destruction of Troy, partially used by Shakespeare in the construction of Troilus and Cressida, 1596; the History of Tom Drum, 1598, alluded to in All's Well that Ends Well; the unique work by Morley, 1600, with the only known contemporary copy of the original music to a song in As You Like It; the Rape of Lucrece, 1624; Love's Labour's Lost, 1598. To these may be added the unique 1568 impression of Lily's Shorte Introduction to Grammar, being the edition probably used at the Stratford school during the poet's sojourn at that institution.

The critical study of the poet's text being altogether outside the scope of my design, the few early editions of his works that are herein mentioned have been admitted, generally speaking, by the merest accident. The unique portion of the first edition of the First Part of Henry the Fourth, 1598, No. 19, is one of the chief exceptions. But early notices and the foundation-stories of the plays are included, these belonging to the history of his work.

Amongst the numerous articles that illustrate the history and topography of Stratford-on-Avon may be mentioned the Clopton cartulary, No. 1; the ground-plan of the College, temp. Hen. 8, No. 221; the interesting perambulation of the town, 1591, No. 222; two curious old levies, No. 248; the earliest books of the manorial court that are known to exist, Nos. 67 and 68; a plan of the town made in 1759, the earliest complete one yet discovered, No. 580; and Fisher's original drawings of the singularly curious paintings discovered on the walls of the Guild Chapel in 1804. These last-mentioned works are of considerable value, the published copies not being strictly accurate, and they are now unique, the only replicas that were made having been lost in the disastrous accident that befell the Staunton collection.

Shakespeare having been as much of a Londoner as he was a Stratfordian, great attention has been paid to the acquisition of plans and views relating to the contemporary metropolis. Amongst these one of the most interesting is Norden's engraving of London Bridge, 1597, described at No. 238. It is the earliest authentic large view of the bridge in the state in which it must necessarily have been familar to the great dramatist. Braun's plan of the city, 1574, in the original state of the plate before the Royal Exchange was introduced, No. 529, is of great rarity, as is also Harrison's view, 1604, No. 292, while the edition of Visscher, No. 162, is unique.

It having been decisively ascertained that Shakespeare was intimately acquainted with Windsor, a considerable number of views of that town have been admitted. Herne's Oak has also received its due meed of attention. In Collier's map, 1742, No. 324, there is the first extrinsic notice of the tree, and a description of the earliest known view, an original drawing by Rooke, will be found at No. 420.

Some of the manuscripts of the Rev. Joseph Greene, who was master of the grammar-school of Stratford-on-Avon from 1746 to 1787, and who was the first antiquary the town has produced, are of considerable interest and include valuable information nowhere else to be found. They were purchased by me, in 1873, from his descendant, the late Richard Greene, F.S.A. About the same time I acquired from the late Joseph Lilly, the well-known bookseller, a copy of the first edition of Dugdale's Antiquities of Warwickshire, 1656, which had belonged to Richard Greene of Lichfield, a person who was intimately connected with Stratford-upon-Avon, and who had illustrated that fine old work with original drawings made by himself and others between the years 1760 and 1769. It was thus that I became possessed of the inestimable earliest representation of the Birth-Place known to exist, and of various drawings executed during that period, all of which are unique; but a sketch of the Jubilee Amphitheatre of 1769, the only contemporary one that has yet been discovered, I gave to the Birth-Place Museum as an article of essential local interest. With that exception the whole of the original illustrations that were found in the volume have been added to the present collection.

There is a variety of articles not readily classified, such as the unique copy of the Return from Parnassus, 1602, No. 37, the only manuscript of the time of Elizabeth in a private library in which any of the works of Shakespeare are mentioned; several early manuscript miscellanies of Shakespearean interest; the important original plan of Middlesex executed by Norden about the year 1593, No. 352; and the first, also the unique, edition of Foole vpon Foole, 1600, No. 751.

Amongst the pieces of theatrical interest may be mentioned the all but unique tract of 1588, No. 56, containing the notice of The Theatre;

the original edition of Roscius Anglicanus, No. 61; the old play-bill, one of the earliest known, No. 229; the rare tract by Field on the accident at Paris Garden, 1583; the unique fragment of a contemporary prompt-copy of Marlowe's Massacre of Paris, No. 287; Gosson's Playes Confuted, No. 285; the original certificate respecting the Blackfriars Theatre, No. 198; the annotated copy of Spenser identifying Tarlton as the "pleasant Willy," No. 3; the interesting document respecting the locality of the Globe Theatre, No. 245; the earliest engraving of Shakespearean characters in a theatre, No. 764.

The artistic portion of the present collection, although so singularly extensive, is not the result of a mere desire for accumulation. It has been formed with the definite purpose of illustrating the Life of Shakespeare by representations of every morsel that could be found of his own contemporary England,—that is to say, of every object that he himself was likely to have seen. Deeply impressed by the rapidity with which these vestiges were disappearing, I engaged Mr. J. T. Blight, F.S.A., a very accomplished draughtsman, to make sketches in furtherance of this design during the years from 1862 to 1868. Not only was every corner of Stratford-upon-Avon and its neighbourhood explored, but we followed as far as we could the routes known to have been taken by the poet in his various journeys, anxiously searching for remains that could be positively assigned to his own times, and carefully excluding those which had passed through the hands of the modern restorer.

I made the acquaintance of Mr. Blight at his native town of Penzance in 1860, an acquaintance which soon ripened into a warm friendship that terminated only with his death to the world through a grievous and incurable malady. A thorough good fellow in every sense of the word, he was also a most agreeable companion, his conversation teeming with quaint and original thought, while he wisely refrained, out of working-hours, from that perpetual chatter on literature and art which some students consider it necessary to maintain, but which, to say the least, does not always act as a restorative. As an archæological draughtsman he was unrivalled in accuracy, taking infinite pains with unlimited patience to secure the representation of the minutest details. That accuracy has added immeasurably to the value of the numerous sketches from his pencil that enrich the present collection, and it is not too much to say, so many of the objects of his work having since been either modernized or destroyed, that no artistic monograph Life of Shakespeare could be complete without the insertion of a large proportion of his drawings.

A large work on the lines above indicated could hardly fail to be welcome to the student, but, as is so often the case, the time occupied in gathering together the necessary artistic and literary material has practically excluded the collector himself from the opportunity of making an effective use of his accumulations. As our Brighton whip, in the old days of coaching, used to say,— "tempus will fudgit,"—and it has fudgited with me until there is but a little working slice of it left. That slice is insufficient for the due execution of such an undertaking. In a very few years, half a century will have elapsed since my first work on Shakespeare was published, and the termination of that period must also, if I survive, be that of my student-work. If the fate of the Archbishop of Grenada is to be escaped, this should be the resolve not merely of those who have traversed the higher walks of literature, but of the lesser votaries, who, like myself, lay claim to nothing beyond a capacity for research and the ability of utilizing its products.

Little autobiographical reflections of this kind might anyhow be excused in a privately-printed brochure of very limited circulation, but they are in fact given as the most effectual method of advising a younger enthusiast that he can, without lack of courtesy to the originator, carry out an important design. When such a one arises with the large means that will be requisite to complete the work in a satisfactory manner, the artistic and other materials that are briefly described in the following pages cannot fail to prove of essential service

J. O. HALLIWELL-PHILLIPPS.

Hollingbury Copse, Brighton,
29 June, 1887.

A CALENDAR.

The arrangement here adopted follows that in which the articles are placed in the cases or volumes, no regard being paid to chronological or other order.

1. The original cartulary, compiled in the time of Henry the Eighth, of the Cloptons of Stratford-on-Avon and Clopton. A folio volume in the ancient vellum covers with leather fastenings. This manuscript, the most important record of the family known to exist, contains numerous interesting notices of Stratford-on-Avon, including two respecting that which was afterwards the Shakespearean estate of New Place. The dates run from 1313 to 1515.

2. Collections respecting the Free-school of Stratford-on-Avon, by the Rev. Joseph Greene, the head-master; the original manuscript written about the year 1760. 4to.

3. Spenser's Faerie Qveene, 1609, and the Shepheards Calender, 1611, with manuscript notes, some of which are extremely interesting, especially the one which identifies Tarlton as the "pleasant Willy." They were written either in

or about the year 1628, as appears from the memorandum at the bottom of the first title. The printed book is not complete, but this is a matter of no importance, its special value resting solely on the manuscript additions.

4. The Rape of Lucrece, by Mr. William Shakespeare. Newly Reuised: London, printed by I. B. for Roger Iackson, and are to be sold at his shop neere the Conduit in Fleet-street, 1624. 12mo.—Of great rarity, not more than one or two other copies being known to exist.

5. A paper in the hand-writing of the Rev. Joseph Greene, Master of the Grammar School of Stratford-on-Avon, 1767, containing the only account of Shakespeare's residence of New Place that has been recorded from the spoken words of a person who had actually seen the building, one Richard Grimmitt, who was born at Stratford in January, 1683, and who "said he in his youth had been a playfellow with Edward Clopton, senior, eldest son of Sir John Clopton, knt., and had been often with him in the great house near the chapel in Stratford call'd New Place; that, to the best of his remembrance, there was a brick wall next the street, with a kind of porch at that end of it next the Chapel, when they cross'd a small kind of green court before they enter'd the house, which was bearing to the left and fronted with brick, with plain windows consisting of common panes of glass set in lead."

6. The View of the House where Shakespear dy'd, since pulled down by Frank Gastrill. A drawing by T. Sharp, of mulberry-tree notoriety, taken by him from some older sketch, c. 1770.

7. New Place, Chapel, Guild-hall, &c., drawn by R. B. Wheler, engraved by F. Eginton, 1806.—Stratford-on-Avon, Street View, Shakespeare's Hall, New Place Garden, Guild Chapel, &c., published by Henry Merridew, Coventry.

8. The most excellent Historie of the Merchant of Venice, with the extreame crueltie of Shylocke the Iewe towards the said Merchant in cutting a just pound of his flesh, and the obtaining of Portia by the choice of three Chests. As it hath beene divers times acted by the Lord Chamberlaine his Servants. Written by William Shakespeare. London, printed by M. P. for Laurence Hayes, and are to be sold at his shop on Fleetbridge. 1637.—Quarto.

9. The True Tragedie of Richarde Duke of Yorke, and the death of good King Henry the sixt, with the whole contention betweene the two Houses, Lancaster and Yorke, as it was sundry times acted by the Right Honourable the Earle of Pembroke his seruantes. Printed at London by W. W. for Thomas Millington, and are to be sold at his shoppe vnder Saint Peters Church in Cornewall, 1600. Two leaves in sheet E. are in facsimile. This is the second edition of the surreptitious copy of the Third Part of Henry the Sixth. Only about six copies known. Quarto.

10. The First Part of the True and Honourable History of the Life of Sir John Oldcastle, the good Lord Cobham. Written by William Shakespeare. 4to. 1600.—A play impudently ascribed by the publisher to the great dramatist, an evidence of the early commercial value of his name.

11. A Wittie and Pleasant Comedie called the Taming of the Shrew. As it was acted by his Maiesties Seruants at the Blacke Friers and the Globe. Written by Will. Shakespeare. London, printed by W. S. for Iohn Smethwicke, and are to be sold at his Shop in Saint Dunstones Churchyard vnder the Diall. 1631.—Quarto.

12. The xv. Bookes of P. Ouidius Naso, entytuled Metamorphosis, translated oute of Latin into English meeter by Arthur Golding, gentleman, a worke very pleasaunt and delectable, 1567. Imprynted at London by Willyam Seres. 4to.—One of the few books that can be positively asserted to have been at least partially read by Shakespeare, several passages from it being adopted in the Tempest.

13. The Life and Death of King Richard the Second, with new Additions of the Parliament Scene and the Deposing of King Richard. As it hath beene acted by the Kings Majesties Servants at the Globe. By William Shakespeare. London, printed by Iohn Norton, 1634.—Quarto.

14. An Apology for Actors containing three briefe Treatises. Written by Thomas Heywood. 4to. 1612.—The postscript contains Heywood's interesting note respecting the attribution to Shakespeare of the Passionate Pilgrim, and the annoyance that its publication inflicted on the latter.

15. The Most Royall and Honourable Entertainement of the famous and renowned King Christiern the Fourth, King of Denmarke, who, with a fleet of gallant ships, arriued on Thursday the 16 day of July, 1606, in Tylbery-Hope, neere

Grauesend. By H. R. At London, 1606.—
England's Farewell to Christian the fourth famous
King of Denmarke, with a relation of such shewes
and seuerall pastimes presented to his Maiestie, as
well at Court the fift day of August last past, as in
other places since his Honourable passage thorow
the Citie of London. By H. Roberts. Printed
at London for William Welby, 1606.—In one
volume, quarto. Shakespeare's company played
three times before the King of Denmark during
the visit herein chronicled.

16. Pierce Penilesse his Supplication to the
Diuell, describing the ouer-spreading of Vice and
suppression of Vertue. Pleasantly interlac'd with
variable delights, and pathetically intermixt with
conceited reproofes. Written by Thomas Nash,
gentleman. London, imprinted by Richard
Ihones, dwelling at the Signe of the Rose and
Crowne, nere Holburne Bridge, 1592.—There
were two editions issued in this year, the present
being the excessively rare first and surreptitious one
which was entered at Stationers' Hall on August
the 8th, 1592. It is of singular interest in its
earliest allusion to any of the works of Shakespeare
that is to be found in our printed or other literature. Quarto. Only one other perfect copy
known.

17. Palladis Tamia, Wits Treasury, being the
second part of Wits Common Wealth, by Francis
Meres, Maister of Artes of both Universities.
At London, printed by P. Short for Cuthbert
Burbie, and are to be sold at his shop at the
Royall Exchange, 1598.—This curious and inte-
resting little volume contains the earliest list of
Shakespeare's works known to exist. 12mo.

18. The Battell of Alcazar fought in Barbarie betweene Sebastian King of Portugall, and Abdelmelec, King of Marocco. 4to. Lond. 1594.—This is one of the very few contemporary plays that are distinctly quoted by Shakespeare.

19. A fragment of four leaves only, but unique, no other vestige of a copy having yet been discovered, of the first edition of the first part of the Hystorie of Henry the Fourth. 1598.—The last line is the only existing record of the true reading in Poins's speech—" How the *fat* rogue roar'd !", and it is something at this late day to recover even one lost word of the immortal text.

20. The First Booke of Ayres, or Little Short Songs to Sing and Play to the Lute, with the base Viole. Newly published by Thomas Morley, Bachiler of Musicke, and one of the Gent. of her Maiesties Royall Chappel. Imprinted at London in litle S. Helen's by William Barley, the assigne of Thomas Morley, and are to be sold at his house in Gracious Streete, 1600. Folio.— Although imperfect, this book is unique, and it is of peculiar value and interest as containing the only known contemporary copy of the original music to the song, " It was a lover and his lass," in As You Like It.

21. A Pleasant Conceited Comedie called Loues labors lost. As it was presented before her Highnes this last Christmas. Newly corrected and augmented by W. Shakespere. Imprinted at London by W. W. for Cutbert Burby, 1598.—Quarto. This is the earliest work of Shakespeare in which his name occurs on a title-page. Three leaves of the text are in facsimile

but all the rest, including the title, is in an exceptionally fine condition, as clean and fresh as when it first issued from the press.

22. The Birth of Merlin, or the Childe hath found his Father. As it hath been several times acted with great applause. Written by William Shakespear and William Rowley. London, printed by Tho. Johnson for Francis Kirkman and Henry Marsh, and are to be sold at the Princes Arms in Chancery-Lane, 1662.—Quarto.

23. A Letter whearin part of the entertainment vntoo the Queenz Maiesty at Killingwoorth Castl in Warwik Sheer in this Soomerz Progress, 1575, iz signified; from a freend officer attendant in the Coourt vnto hiz freend a Citizen and Merchaunt of London. Small octavo.—The original black-letter edition.

24. The Teares of the Isle of Wight shed on the Tombe of their most noble, valorous and louing Captaine and Governour, the right Honourable Henric, Earle of Southampton, who dyed in the Netherlands, Nouemb. 10, at Bergen-vp-Zone. Printed at London by William Iones, dwelling in Red-crosse-streete, 1625.—Quarto.

25. The right excellent and famous Historye of Promos and Cassandra, wherein is showne the unsufferable abuse of a lewde Magistrate, the vertuous behaviour of a chaste Ladye, &c., the worke of George Whetstones, gent. Imprinted at London by Richarde Ihones, and are to be solde ouer agaynst Saint Sepulchres Church, without Newgate, August 20, 1578.—This is the play whence Shakespeare derived the plot of Measure for Measure. Only three other copies known.

26. The Historie of Henry the Fourth, with the Battell at Shrewsbury betweene the King and Lord Henry Percy, surnamed Henry Hotspur of the North. With the humorous conceits of Sir Iohn Falstaffe. Newly corrected by William Shake-speare. London, Printed by John Norton, and are to be sold by Hvgh Perry at his shop next to Ivie-bridge in the Strand, 1639.—4to.

27. The Raigne of King Edward the Third, as it hath bene sundry times played about the Citie of London. Imprinted at London by Simon Stafford for Cuthbert Burby, and are to be sold at his shop neere the Royall Exchange, 1599.— A play generally believed to have been revised by Shakespeare.

28. Timbre de Cardone ende Fenicie van Messine, a Dutch play on the story of Much Ado about Nothing acted in Holland in the year 1618, with a wood-engraving of one of the scenes. Mr. E. W. Gosse, in a long and interesting article on this drama which appeared in the Athenæum of 10 Nov. 1877, observes,—" in the year after Shakespeare died, the Dutch poet wrote his tragi-comedy of Timbre de Cardone, in which it appears to me that he made large use of his reminiscences of Much Ado about Nothing. The next year saw its publication.—This excessively rare play, which was at one time thought to have entirely disappeared, and which has never been reprinted, is so interesting, both intrinsically and to Shake-spearean scholars, that I may be permitted to describe it somewhat minutely. The title runs :— ' J. J. Starter's Blyeyndich-Truyrspel van Timbre de Cardone ende Fenicie van Messine,' or, in English, 'J. J. Starter's Tragi-comedy of Timbre

de Cardone and Fenicie of Messine.' The title-page has an engraving of Gironde pointing out the supposed tomb of Fenicie to Timbre in the church. The imprint states that the play is printed 'for Jan Jensen Starter, Bookseller at the Sign of the English Bible, in Leeuwarden, 1618, 4to. There is an interesting prologue, in which Starter refers with modest enthusiasm to his great contemporaries, and deprecates comparison with them."

29. Lily's Shorte Introduction of Grammar generally to be used, compiled and set forth for the bringing up of all those that intende to attaine the knowledge of the Latine tongue. 4to. Lond. 1568.—An impression which is either unique or of very extreme rarity, being unnoticed by all the bibliographers. It is, in all probability, either this edition or that of 1567, also in this collection, which was in use at the Stratford grammar-school when Shakespeare was gathering his "little Latin and less Greek" at that establishment. That the great dramatist had imbibed something from this book is clear from his quoting a line from Terence in the form in which it is given in this volume, not in that in which it appears in the work of the ancient poet.

30. Microcosmos, the Discovery of the Little World, with the Government thereof. By John Davies. At Oxford, printed by Ioseph Barnes, and are to bee solde in Fleetestreete at the signe of the Turkes head by Iohn Barnes, 1603. 4to. —At p. 215 are the curious allusions to Shake-speare and Burbage, the identification proved by their initials in the margin.

31. Poems, written by Wil. Shake-speare gent. Printed at London by Tho. Cotes, and are to be sold by Iohn Benson, dwelling in St. Dunstans Church-yard, 1640. 12mo.—With both title-pages, one being undated, and with Marshall's original engraved portrait of the author, an interesting variation of Droeshout's work.

32. The History of the Two Maids of More-clacke (Mortlake), with the Life and simple manner of John in the Hospitall. Written by Robert Armin, Shakespeare's colleague, 1609.—The woodcut on the title-page is one of the few pictorial examples that we have of the stage costume of Shakespeare's time. Only four other copies known.

33. Loues Labours Lost, a wittie and pleasant Comedie, as it was acted by his Maiesties Seruants at the Blacke-Friers and the Globe. Written by William Shakespeare. London, printed by W. S. for Iohn Smethwicke, and are to be sold at his Shop in Saint Dunstones Churchyard vnder the Diall, 1631.—Quarto.

34. The Booke of Honor of Armes, wherein is discoursed the causes of Quarrell and the nature of Iniuries, with their repulses. Also the meanes of satisfaction and pacification. No date, but entered on the Stationers' registers in 1589.—Quarto. A book, so far as observations on "lies" are concerned, similar to the one mentioned in the next article.

35. Vincentio Saviolo his Practise. In two Bookes. The first intreating of the use of the Rapier and Dagger. The second, of Honor and honorable Quarrels. 4to. London, printed by

John Wolfe, 1595.—This book is alluded to by Touchstone in As You Like It.—" O, sir, we quarrel in print by the book," &c.

36. The head of Shakespeare in an oval 1655, evidently copied from the Droeshout print, only reversed. Under it is a representation on the stage, with the figures of a man and woman, the latter in the act of stabbing herself. Will: Gilbirson, John Stafford excud.—A modern reproduction of this engraving is sufficiently common, but the present is a very fine specimen of the extremely rare original. Only four other copies known.

37. A manuscript of the Return from Parnassus, "as it was acted in St. John's Colledge in Cambridge, anno 1602."—This is the only manuscript of the time of Elizabeth in a private library in which any of the works of Shakespeare are mentioned. It is of great interest and literary value as the record of a more accurate text than the hitherto only known early copy, the edition of 1606. The title in the manuscript is " the Progresse to Parnassus," the reason for the adoption of either title being obscure.—4to.

38. The Auncient Historie of the Destruction of Troy, containing the founders and foundation of the said Citie, besides many admirable and most rare exployts of chivalric and martiall prowesse, with incredible events compassed for and through the love of ladies. 4to. London, printed by Thomas Creede, 1596.—This is the edition which was used by Shakespeare for a portion of the story of Troilus and Cressida. Only one other copy known, and both are imperfect.

39. M. William Shake-speare, his True Chronicle History of the life and death of King Lear and his three Daughters; with the vnfortunate life of Edgar, sonne and heire to the Earle of Glocester, and his sullen and assumed humour of Tom of Bedlam, as it was plaid before the Kings Maiesty at White-Hall vppon S. Stephens night in Christmas Hollidaies. By his Maiesties Seruants playing vsually at the Globe on the Banck-side. Printed for Nathaniel Butter. 1608.—4to.

40. The history of Tom Drum's vaunts, and his rare entertainment at Mistress Farmer's house, the faire widow of Fleete Streete. A fragment of Deloney's Historie of the Gentle Craft, 1598.—Alluded to in All's Well that Ends Well. No other copy known.

41. Hollands Leagver, or an Historical Discovrse of the Life and Actions of Dona Britanica Hollandia, the Arch-Mistris of the wicked women of Evtopia; wherein is detected the notorious Sinne of Panderisme, and the execrable Life of the luxurious Impudent. London, printed by A. M. for Richard Barnes, 1632.—Quarto. Curious references to the Globe Theatre and other Shakespearean localities. With the original engraved frontispiece.

42. The original correspondence and papers of the Rev. Joseph Greene, Master of the Grammar-School of Stratford-on-Avon, 1746 to 1787, including numerous documents concerning the restoration of the poet's monumental effigy in 1748, the prologue to Othello acted by John Ward's Company in aid of the restoration fund, with an autograph letter from Ward to Greene respecting the monument, &c. 4to. MS.

43. Complaints. Containing sundrie small Poemes of the World's Vanitie. London. Imprinted for William Ponsonbie, dwelling in Paules Churchyard at the signe of the Bishops Head, 1591.—Quarto. The allusion to "our pleasant Willy" is at sig. F. 2.

44. The Garden of the Muses. Printed at London by E. A. for Iohn Tap, and are to be sold at his shop at Saint Magnus corner, 1610.— This little volume is a collection of passages from the works of Shakespeare and other poets. 12mo.

45. The Most Excellent and Lamentable Tragedie of Romeo and Juliet, as it hath been sundry times publikely Acted by the Kings Majesties Servants at the Globe. Written by W. Shake-speare. Newly corrected, augmented, and amended. London, Printed by R. Young for John Smethwicke, and are to be sold at his Shop in St. Dunstans Church-yard in Fleetstreet under the Dyall, 1637.—4to.

46. The Late and much-admired Play called Pericles, Prince of Tyre. With the true Relation of the whole History, adventures, and fortunes of the said Prince. Written by W. Shakespeare. Printed at London by Thomas Cotes, 1635.—4to.

47. A Declaration of egregious Popish Impostures, to with-draw the harts of her Maiesties Subiects from their allegeance, and from the truth of Christian Religion professed in England, vnder the pretence of casting out deuils. At London, printed by Iames Roberts dwelling in Barbican, 1603.—The first edition of a book that was in Shakespeare's recollection when he composed his tragedy of Lear. 4to.

48. Colin Clovt's Come Home Againe. By Ed. Spencer. London, printed for William Ponsonbie, 1595. — At sig. C. 2 is the allusion to Shakespeare under the name of Aetion. 4to.

49. The True Chronicle Historie of the whole Life and Death of Thomas Lord Cromwell, as it hath beene sundry times publikely Acted by the Kings Maiesties Seruants. Written by W. S. London, printed by Thomas Snodham, 1613. Quarto.

50. Every Man in his Humor, as it hath beene sundry times publickly acted by the right Honorable the Lord Chamberlaine his seruants. Written by Ben. Iohnson. Imprinted at London for Walter Burre, and are to be sould at his shoppe in Paules Church-yarde, 1601.—Quarto. Shakespeare was one of the actors in this comedy when it was originally produced in 1598.

51. Englandes Mourning Garment, worne here by plaine Shepheardes in memorie of their sacred Mistresse Elizabeth, Queene of Vertue while shee liued, and Theame of Sorrow, being dead. Printed at London by V. S. for Thomas Millington, and are to be sold at his shop vnder Saint Peters Church in Cornhil.—Quarto. By Henry Chettle, who introduces in the poetical division a plaintive allusion to Shakespeare. Two leaves at the end, containing the Shepherd's Spring Song, are wanting in this as in several of the few other known copies.

52. The original manuscript poetical commonplace-book of Matthew Day, a prominent inhabitant of Windsor in the first half of the seventeenth century. He was five times mayor of that town;

and died in 1661. It includes, amidst a large number of other pieces, verses of "Shakespeare on the King"; lines on persons buried at Windsor; on Richard Pipe; on the cornell tree in the Little Parke; Randolph on the losse of his little finger; Paul his Temple triumphant, or a new walke there vp the steppes, by Tho. Dekker; a new Ballad of the Dauncing of the Ropes, by Tho. Decker; on the goodwif's ale, &c. Quarto.

53. The Whole Contention betweene the two Famous Houses, Lancaster and Yorke. With the Tragicall ends of the good Duke Humfrey, Richard Duke of Yorke and King Henrie the sixt. Diuided into two Parts, and newly corrected and enlarged. Written by William Shakespeare, gent. Printed at London for T. P.—Quarto. There is no date in the original, but it was printed in 1619.

54. The Merry Conceited Humors of Bottom the Weaver. As it hath been often publikely Acted by Some of his Majesties Comedians, and lately privately presented by several Apprentices for their harmless recreation with great Applause. London, printed for F. Kirkman and H. Marsh, 1661.—Quarto.

55. A Yorkshire Tragedie, not so New as Lamentable and True. Written by W. Shakespeare. Printed for T. P., 1619.—Quarto.

56. A Trve Report of the Inditement, Arraignment, conuiction, condemnation, and execution of Iohn Weldon, William Hartley and Robert Sutton, who suffred for High Treason in seuerall places about the Citie of London on Saturday the fifth of October, anno 1588. Imprinted at London by

Richard Iones, 1588.—Quarto. Hartley was executed "nigh the Theater" in Shoreditch.

57. The Merry Divel of Edmonton, as it hath beene sundry times Acted by his Maiesties Seruants at the Globe on the Banke-side. At London, printed by G. Eld for Arthur Iohnson, dwelling at the signe of the White Horse in Paules Churchyard over against the great North Doore of Paules, 1617.—Quarto.

58. The Malcontent, augmented by Marston. With the Additions played by the Kings Maiesties Servants. Written by Ihon Webster, 1604. At London, printed by V. S. for William Aspley, and are to be sold at his shop in Paules Churchyard.—Quarto. This edition contains the induction in which the Shakespearean actors are introduced.

59. Satiro-Mastix, or the Vntrussing of the Humorous Poet. As it hath bin presented publikely by the Right Honorable the Lord Chamberlaine his Seruants, and priuately by the Children of Paules. By Thomas Dekker. London, printed for Edward White, and are to bee solde at his shop neere the little North doore of Paules Church, at the signe of the Gun, 1602.—Quarto. Includes notices of the Comedy of Errors and Justice Shallow.

60. One of the volumes of Ireland's pseudo-Shakespearean library, in the same binding, green morocco, in which it was sold at his sale in May, 1801, lot 566. Some of the forged notes are very quaint, especially a delicious one at p. 9,—"werte notte for those who dydde give mee thys booke, I would reade noe more ont."

61. Roscius Anglicanus, or an Historical Review of the Stage after it had been suppress'd by means of the late unhappy Civil War, giving an Account of its rise again, of the times and places the Governours of both the Companies first erected their theatres, the names of the principal Actors and Actresses, &c. 12mo. Lond. 1708.

62. The Tragedy of Hamlet, Prince of Denmarke, newly imprinted and inlarged, according to the true and perfect copy lastly Printed. By William Shakespeare. London, printed by W. S. for Iohn Smethwicke, and are to be sold in his Shop in Saint Dunstans Church-yard in Fleet-street vnder the Diall.—Quarto.

63. The Late and much admired Play called, Pericles, Prince of Tyre. With the true Relation of the whole History, aduentures, and fortunes of the saide Prince. Written by W. Shakespeare. Printed for T. P., 1619.—Quarto.

64. The Two Noble Kinsmen, presented at the Blackfriers by the Kings Maiesties servants with great applause. Written by the memorable Worthies of their time, Mr. John Fletcher and Mr. William Shakspeare, gent. Printed at London by Tho. Cotes for Iohn Waterson, and are to be sold at the signe of the Crowne in Pauls Church-yard, 1634.—Quarto.

65. The most excellent Historie of the Merchant of Venice, with the extreame cruelty of Shylocke the Jew towards the said Merchant in cutting a just pound of his flesh, and the obtaining of Portia by the choyce of three Chests. As it hath been diverse times acted by the Lord Chamberlaine his Servants. Written by William Shakespeare.

London, printed for William Leake, and are to be solde at his shop at the signe of the Crown in Fleetstreet, between the two Temple Gates. 1652.—Quarto.

66. The Retvrne from Pernassvs, or the Scourge of Simony. Publiquely acted by the Students in Saint Iohns Colledge in Cambridge. At London, printed by G. Eld for Iohn Wright, and are to bee sold at his shop at Christchurch Gate, 1606.—Quarto. The well-known allusions to Shakespeare occur at sig. B. 2 and sig. G. 2. In this impression the word *lazy* is omitted in the verses on his poems. The following contemporary manuscript note occurs upon the title-page,—"to my lovinge Smallocke, J. D."

67. The original Presentments and Orders made at the Court Leets of Stratford-on-Avon from 1682 to 1743. A manuscript volume, in folio, of extreme interest in its notices of the condition of the town and the usages of the inhabitants during that period. It includes occasional allusions to Shakespearean localities and autograph signatures of some of the Hathaways.

68. The original court-book, with presentments, of Old Stratford from 1684 to 1697. Manuscript, in folio, with the primitive vellum covers. It includes curious notices of the Shakespearean common-fields.

69. The Droeshout engraved portrait of Shakespeare, an unnoticed impression which was issued by Herringman in 1672 from the plate used in the third folio of 1664. No other copy known.

70. A Treatise concerneinge the tenure of Coppy holders, teachinge bothe Lorde and

Tennant how to demeane them in all sortes, very necessarye for eyther of ther vses to be had and understood.—Dedicated by its author, Philip Chapman, "to the Right Worshipfull Sir Thomas Lucye, knight, his singuler good master, and the right vertuous and his very good lady, the Lady Constance his wife." This was the son of the poet's Sir Thomas. A minute beautifully-written manuscript, in the original impressed vellum binding. 18mo. Temp. Jac. I.

71. Tragi-Comædia, being a Brief Relation of the strange and wonderfull hand of God discovered at Witny in the Comedy acted there February the third, where there were some slaine, many hurt, with severall other remarkable Passages. By John Rowe of C. C. C. in Oxford, Lecturer in the Towne of Witny. Oxford, printed by L. Lichfield for Henry Cripps, 1653.—A singularly curious account of an accident that happened at the White Hart inn, Witney, during the performance of the comedy of Mucedorus by some itinerant players. 4to.

72. The Ancient Historie of the Destruction of Troy, conteining the Founders and Foundation of the said Citie. Translated out of French into English by W. Caxton. Newly corrected, and the English much amended, by William Fiston. London, printed by Thomas Creede, 1607.—The title-pages and Shakespearean portions only. Quarto.

73. A Declaration of egregious Popish Impostures to withdraw the harts of his Maiesties Subiects from their allegeance, and from the truth of Christian Religion professed in England, vnder the pretence of casting out of deuils. At London,

printed by Iames Roberts, dwelling in Barbican, Anno Dom. 1604.—A re-issue of extreme rarity. 4to. It was from this book that Shakespeare adopted the names of spirits mentioned in his tragedy of Lear.

74. A Shorte Introduction of Grammar generally to be vsed, compiled and set forth for the bringing vp of all those that intende to attaine the knowledge of the Latine tongue, 1567; Brevissima Institutio, 1567.—Of extreme rarity, and probably unique in this fine perfect state. 4to. Either this or the next year's edition, copies of both of which are in this collection, was most likely the one in use at the Stratford school in the poet's boyhood.

75. Remains of a Greater Worke concerning Britaine, the inhabitants thereof, their Languages, Names, Surnames, Empreses, Wise Speeches, Poesies and Epitaphes. At London, printed by G. E. for Simon Waterson. 1605.—This work contains one of the very few contemporary notices of Shakespeare. 4to.

76. The cover of an old book containing lines from the Lover's Complaint and the Passionate Pilgrim in a hand-writing of the time of Charles the First. 12mo.

77. The History of Titus Andronicus, the renowned Roman General, who, after he had saved Rome by his Valour from being destroyed by the barbarous Goths, and lost two-and-twenty of his valiant sons in ten Years War, was, upon the Emperor's marrying the Queen of the Goths, put to Disgrace and banish'd; but being recall'd, the Emperor's Son by a first Wife was murder'd by

the Empress's Sons and a bloody Moor, and how, charging it upon Andronicus's sons, tho' he cut off his hand to redeem their lives, they were murder'd in Prison. How his fair daughter Lavinia, being ravish'd by the Empress's Sons, they cut out her Tongue and Hands off, &c. How Andronicus slew them, made Pyes of their Flesh, and presented them to the Emperor and Empress; and then slew them also. With the miserable Death he put the wicked Moor to; then, at her Request, slew his Daughter and himself to avoid Torments. Newly translated from the Italian copy printed at Rome. London, printed and sold by C. Dicey in Bow Church-yard, and at his wholesale Warehouse in Northampton.—Of singular rarity. It is probably a chap-book version of the prose tale of Titus Andronicus, which was popular in Shakespeare's time, but of which no copy is now known to exist.

78. The original memorandum book of Thomas Sharp, the clock-maker of Stratford-on-Avon, who purchased the wood of Shakespeare's mulberry-tree when it was cut down in the middle of the last century. This manuscript came afterwards into the hands of Sharp's only surviving assistant, Thomas Gibbs, whose note at p. 186 shows how he came into the possession of some pieces of the mulberry-wood, the few remaining portions of which were purchased by me at the sale of his effects in the year 1866. 12mo.

79. A small piece of the wood of Shakespeare's mulberry-tree, interesting as being an unworked fragment as it must have originally appeared, nearly all the bark still remaining. This is one of the few bits of the wood that are mentioned in the preceding article as having been in the possession

of Thomas Gibbs at the time of his decease. He died in 1866, aged 84.

80. A small tea-caddy, one of the best specimens extant of Sharp's carved-work from the wood of the poet's mulberry-tree, with the original stamped note,—" Shakespear's Wood, Sharp, Stratford-on-Avon." Sharp purchased the wood about the year 1759, and traded in relics made from it until his death in 1799, but the present specimen has every appearance of belonging to one of the earlier years of that period. Five inches long, $3\frac{1}{2}$ wide, 4 deep.

81. An interesting account of Shakespeare's Birth-Place written by the late F. W. Fairholt immediately after his first visit to the spot in the year 1839. Autograph and unpublished. 8vo.

82.—New Shreds of the Old Snare, containing the Apparitions of two new female Ghosts. By John Gee, Master of Arts, late of Exon Colledge in Oxford. London, printed for Robert Mylbourne, 1624.—Curious allusions to Hamlet and the Midsummer Night's Dream at p. 20. 4to.

83. The Manner of the Proceedings of Robert Earle of Essex, and Henry Earle of Southampton, with their Arreignement. The Speaches of Ro: Earle of Essex, with his Poem, before his execution. Letters, together with their answeres, sent vnto the Earle of Essex by my Lord Keeper and others. Diuers Speeches against the Earle of Essex and his proceedings in Ireland. 1601. Written by Francis ap Rice, and by him approued of.—A neatly written contemporary manuscript, some of the most curious portions of which are unpublished. See extracts from it in the Outlines

of the Life of Shakespeare, ed. 1886, i., 178-182.
In quarto.

84. The Conquest of Granada by the Spaniards, in two Parts; acted at the Theater Royall. Written by John Dryden, Servant to His Majesty. In the Savoy. 1672.—Contains the traditional account of Shakespeare's treatment of the character of Mercutio and various other notices of the great dramatist. 4to.

85. Titus Andronicus, or the Rape of Lavinia. Acted at the Theatre Royall. A Tragedy alter'd from Mr. Shakespears Works by Mr. Edw. Ravenscroft. London, 1687.—4to. The address to the reader contains the assumed traditional notice of the original authorship.

86. The Orator, handling a hundred seuerall Discourses in forme of Declamations; some of the Arguments being drawne from Titus Livius and other ancient Writers, the rest of the Authors owne inuention; part of which are of matters happened in our Age. Written in French by Alexander Siluayn, and Englished by L. P. London, printed by Adam Islip, 1596.—Declamation 95, of a Jew who would for his debt haue a pound of the flesh of a Christian, and the Christian's answere. 4to.

87. Macbeth, a Tragedy, with all the Alterations, Amendments, Additions, and New Songs. As it is now Acted at the Dukes Theatre, 1674. Quarto.

88. The Tempest, or the Enchanted Island, a Comedy, as it is now Acted at His Highness the Duke of York's Theatre, 1670 and 1674. Two

vols., 4to. These editions differ materially from each other, but they both contain the interesting notice of the performance of the drama at the Blackfriars. The later issues follow, I believe, the second of these editions.

89. The Comical Gallant, or the Amours of Sir John Falstaffe, a Comedy, as it is Acted at the Theatre Royal in Drury-lane by his Majesty's Servants. By Mr. Dennis. London, printed and sold by A. Baldwin near the Oxford Arms in Warwick-lane, 1702.—4to. With a dedication in which there is the earliest traditional account of the causes which led to the composition of the Merry Wives of Windsor.

90. Verginia, Comedia di M. Bernardo Accolti Aretino, intitolata la Verginia, con un Capitolo della Madonna, nuouamente corretta, et con somma diligentia ristampata. Stampata in Vinegia per Nicolo di Aristotile detto Zoppino, 1535.—A play on the story that was dramatized by Shakespeare in All's Well that Ends Well. 12mo.

91. Epitia Tragedia di M. Gio. Battista Giraldi Cinthio, nobile Ferrarese. In Venetia, appresso Giulio Cesare Cagnacini, 1583.—A play on the story that was afterwards dramatized by Shakespeare in Measure for Measure. 12mo.

92. Naps upon Parnassus, a sleepy Muse nipt and pincht, though not awakened ; such voluntary and jovial Copies of Verses as were lately receiv'd from some of the Wits of the Universities in a Frolick, dedicated to Gondibert's Mistress by Captain Jones and others. London, printed by express Order from the Wits, for N. Brook at the Angel in Cornhill, 1658.—At sig. B. 5 is a

singularly quaint allusion to Shakespeare's Falstaff. Small 8vo.

93. Le Notti di M. Gio. Francesco Straparola da Carauaggio. In Vinegia, 1560, appresso Francesco Lorenzini de Turino.—With the autograph and manuscript notes of Gabriel Harvey, the former being on the title-page of the second part. Interesting in connexion with the history of the foundation-story of the Merry Wives of Windsor, a proof that one copy at all events of this book had found its way into England in Shakespeare's time. Small 8vo.

94. The Pleasant and Delightful History of Dorastus and Fawnia, pleasant for Age to shun drowsie Thoughts, profitable for Youth to avoid other wanton pastimes, and bringing to both a desired content. By Rob. Green, Master of Arts in Cambridge. London, printed by W. O. for G. Conyers at the Ring in Little Britain.—The lower part of the imprint cut off. A curious wood-cut on the title-page. This is a chap-book version of the foundation-story of the Winter's Tale. 12mo. —The History of Dorastus and Fawnia, where is declared the cruelty of Pandosta to his fair Bellaria; and how the child Fawnia was put into a boat to be drown'd, but was taken up by the sea-side out of the boat by a shepherd; and how he brought up the fair Fawnia to keep sheep, and how Dorastus fell in love with the fair Fawnia, &c. London, printed for J. Blare at the Looking-glass on London Bridge.—A quaint wood-cut on the title-page. Substantially perfect, but the right hand of title is slightly cropped. An extremely rare edition of this popular Shakespearean tale. 12mo. In one volume.

95. Cornelianvm Dolium. Comædia lepidissima, optimorum judiciis approbata, et theatrali coryphœo, nec immerito, donata, palma chorali apprime digna. Auctore T. R., ingeniosissimo hujus ævi Heliconio. Londini, apud Tho. Harperum, et væneunt per Tho. Slaterum et Laurentium Chapman, 1638.—With Marshall's frontispiece of the man in the tub. In this curious old Latin play there is an interesting notice of Shakespeare's "wanton book," that is to say, his Venus and Adonis. 12mo.

96. Epigrams Six Bookes, also the Socratick Session, or the Arraignment of Julius Scaliger, with some select Poems, by S. Sheppard. London, printed by G. D., and are to be sould by Tho: Bucknell at the Golden Lion in Duck-lane. 1651.— Epig. 17, in Memory of our Famous Shakespeare. Small 8vo.

97. Cesar Tragedie, par Iaques Grevin de Clermont en Beauuaisis. A Paris, par Nicolas Bonfons, ruë neuue nostre Dame, à l'enseigne sainct Nicolas, 1578.—A French tragedy on the subject of Julius Cæsar. 12mo.

98. An Account of the Lady Lucy, write to a pertickular friend of hers, Mrs. Moore.—This Lady Lucy was the wife of the second Sir Thomas of Charlecote. It was drawn up by Mrs. Elizabeth Lucy, one of her descendants. See an account of this manuscript in Hunter's Illustrations of Shakespeare, i. 61, 62. 12mo.

99. The Passionate Pilgrim, by W. Shakespeare. At London, printed for W. Iaggard and are to be sold by W. Leake at the Greyhound in Paules Churchyard, 1599.—A facsimile tracing

made by E. W. Ashbee from the original printed copy preserved in the Capell collection.

100. Histoires Tragiques extraictes des oevvres Italiennes de Bandel, et mises en nostre langue Françoise par Pierre Boaistuau, surnommé Launay, natif de Bretaigne. A Paris, par Benoist Preuost, rue Frementel, à l'enseigne de l'estoille d'or pres le cloz Bruneau, 1559.—Includes the story of Romeo and Juliet. Small 8vo.

101. The Tragedy of Hamlet, Prince of Denmark, as it is now acted at His Highness the Duke of York's Theatre. By William Shakespeare. London, 1676.—4to.

102. Original drafts of advertisements, letters, and conditions of sale drawn up on the occasion of the projected auction of Shakespeare's Birth-Place in the year 1805.—Fol. MS.

103. Marc Antonio e Cleopatra, tragedia del R. don Celso Pistorelli da Vicenza. In Verona, per Sebastiano dalle Donne, et Giouanni frattelli, 1576.—12mo.

104. The Barrons Wars in the raigne of Edward the Second, with Englands Heroicall Epistles, by Michaell Drayton. At London, printed by I. R. for N. Ling, 1603.—That portion only of the book which contains the prototype of a passage in Shakespeare's Julius Cæsar. 12mo.

105. Julius Cæsar, a Tragedy, as it is now acted at the Theatre Royal. Written by William Shakespeare. London, 1691.—4to.

106. Stanzas on the Shakespeare Hunt at Stratford-upon-Avon, December the 2d, 1793,

illustrated with Notes; humbly inscribed to Charles Henry Hunt, esq., by John Jordan.—Some of the Shakespearean notes are biographical. Autograph manuscript. Fol.

107. The Merry Deuill of Edmonton, as it hath been sundry times acted by his Maiesties Seruants at the Globe on the Bancke-side. London, printed by T. P. for Francis Falkner, and are to be sold at his Shoppe neere vnto S. Margarites-hill in Southwarke, 1631.—4to.

108. Ben Johnsons Ode to Himself; Randolph's Answer to B. J., ode; the Ode in Latine by Mr. Stroude; the same by Thomas Randolph.—A manuscript of the time of Charles the First, containing interesting notices of the drama of Pericles. 12mo.

109. The Hogge hath Lost his Pearle, a Comedy divers Times publikely acted by certaine London Prentices. By Robert Tailor. London, printed by Richard Redmer, and are to be solde at the West dore of Paules, at the signe of the Starre, 1614.—Curious allusion in the Prologue to the drama of Pericles. 4to.

110. Euphues Golden Legacie found after his death in his Cell at Silexedra, bequeathed to Philavtvs Sonnes, nursed vp with their Father in England. Fecht from the Canaries by T. L. Gent. Imprinted at London for Iohn Smethwick, and are to be sold at his shop in Saint Dunstanes Church-yard in Fleet Streete, vnder the Dyall, 1623.—Black-letter. The eighth edition of the popular foundation-story of As You Like It.

111. An Abstract of the several Deeds and Writings relating to the Title of one part of a

messuage or tenement and premises in Stratford-upon-Avon, formerly called the Swann Inn and now the White Lyon Inn, belonging to Mr. John Payton, 1770.—This property adjoins the poet's Birth-Place, and the abstract commences with a notice of a feoffment, dated in 1591, in which there is an allusion to John Shakespeare. Fol. MS.

112. Draft Abstracts of Title to the White Lion Inn and to grounds which adjoin Shakespeare's Birth-Place, c. 1822.—These abstracts are of considerable importance in tracing the history and boundaries of the garden belonging to the Birth-Place. Fol. MS.

113. Rex Platonicus, sive de potentissimi principis Iacobi Britanniarum regis, ad illustrissimam Academiam Oxoniensem, adventu, Aug. 27, anno 1605. Narratio ab Isaaco Wake, Pvblico Academiæ ejusdem Oratore. Oxoniæ, excudebat Iosephus Barnesius, anno Dom. 1607.—Has an account of the interlude on the subject of Macbeth which was performed before King James at Oxford in 1605. 4to.

114. A copy of Shakespeare's Will made about the year 1747 by the Rev. Joseph Greene, of Stratford-on-Avon, taken apparently from an early official copy that had been collated with the original by one Gilbert Rothwell, a public notary.—4to. MS.

115. Original documents respecting Warwickshire families of the name of Shakespeare, sixteenth and seventeenth centuries.—4to. MS.

116. A Levy of Knolle Manor, co. Warw.—A manuscript of the seventeenth century containing

notices of persons of the name of Shakespeare. In octavo.

117. Troilus and Cressida, or Truth Found Too Late, a Tragedy, as it is acted at the Duke's Theatre, to which is Prefix'd a Preface containing the Grounds of Criticism in Tragedy. Written by John Dryden, Servant to His Majesty. London, 1679.—With the rare poetical address to the author by R. Duke. 4to. Dryden's Preface includes much of Shakespearean interest.

118. Julius Cæsar, a Tragedy, as it is now acted at the Theatre Royal. Written by William Shakespeare. London, n.d.—This edition was printed about the year 1695, and the present is a prompter's copy of it, with manuscript notes and alterations made long afterwards, in all probability in the time of Garrick. 4to.

119. La Hadriana, Tragedia Nova, di Lvigi Groto Cieco d'Hadria. Nuouamente ristampata. In Venetia, appresso Fabio et Agostin Zopini fratelli, 1586.—Probably known to the writer of the ancient English play of Romeo and Juliet, the one that was anterior to Shakespeare's tragedy on that subject. 12mo.

120. Othello, the Moor of Venice, a Tragedy, as it hath been divers times acted at the Globe and at the Black-Friers, and now at the Theatre Royal, by his Majesties Servants. Written by William Shakespear. London, 1687.—4to.

121. The Example, as it was Presented by her Majesties Servants at the private House in Drury-Lane. Written by Iames Shirly. London, printed by Iohn Norton for Andrew Crooke and William

Cooke, 1637.—A quotation at sig. C. 4 from Henry the Fourth. 4to.

122. An Account of Plays acted at the New Theatre Royal in Lincolns Inn Fields and at the Theatre Royal in Drury Lane, 1714 to 1723.— The original manuscript chronicle of theatrical performances, including a large number of notices of theatrical and Shakespearean interest. 4to.

123. The Correspondence of the Harts respecting matters connected with Shakespeare's Birth-Place, a collection of original letters, 1793 to 1806. —4to. MS.

124. The original exemplification, on vellum, of a fine that was levied in Michaelmas Term, 23 Car. I., 1647, on Shakespeare's London estate, therein described as *unum mesuagium cum pertinentiis in parochia Sancte Anne, Blackfriers*, 29 November, 23 Car. 1.

125. Counterpart of a Lease, dated 1 December, 1675, granted by Sir Edward Walker, knight, Garter Principall Kinge of Armes, to Joseph Hunt, of Stratford-upon-Avon in the county of Warwick, gent., of "all that messuage with thappurtenances comonly called or knowne by the name of the New Place, scituate, lyinge and beinge in Stratford-upon-Avon aforesaid, in the said county of Warwicke, in a certaine streete there called the Chappell Streete." The original indenture signed by Joseph Hunt.

126. Conveyance from Edward Clopton, of Stratford-upon-Avon, esq., to Hugh Clopton, of Clopton in the county of Warwick, esq., of "all the said seate or pew scituate in the Parish Church of

Stratford aforesaid belonging to the messuage called the New Place," 1 May, 1701.—The original indenture signed by Edward Clopton, witnessed by Sir John Clopton and Nathaniel Mason.

127. Lease for Possession on the Marriage of Hugh Clopton, esq., with Miss Milward, 25 September, 1702, of "all that messuage or tenement, scituate, lyeing and being in the Chappell Street and Chappell Lane, within the burrowe of Stratford-upon-Avon in the county of Warwick, comonly called or known by the name of the New Place, late in the tenure of John Wheeler, gent.," with farms and lands at Clopton, &c. The original indenture signed by Sir John Clopton, Hugh Clopton, Thomas and Anne Milward.

128. Articles of Agreement Tripartite, made, concluded, and fully agreed vpon this six and twentieth day of September, annoque Domini 1702, betweene Sir John Clopton, of Clopton in the county of Warwicke, knight, of the first part, Hugh Clopton, of Clopton aforesaid, in the said county of Warwick, esq., of the second part, and Thomas Millward of Cudworth, in the said county of Warwicke, esq., of the third part. Mentions at length the new mansion then recently erected on the site of Shakespeare's residence at New Place.—The original deed signed by Sir John Clopton, Hugh Clopton, and Thomas Milward.

129. Lease for a year from Edward Clopton, esq., of Stratford-upon-Avon, to Aston Ingram, of Little Woolford, in the county of Warwick, esq., of "all that peece or parcell of ground, lyeing and beeing within the borrough of Stratford-upon-Avon, called or known by the name of the

Great Garden, and which did formerly belong to New Place, and is adjoyning to the now dwelling-house of him, the said Edward Clopton, and conteynes by estimation about three quarters of an acre, bee the same more or less," 21 March, 1705.—The original indenture signed by Edward Clopton.

130. Release from Edward Clopton, esq., of Stratford-upon-Avon, to Aston Ingram, esq., of "the Great Garden, which formerly did belong to New Place," 22 March, 1705.—The original indenture signed by Edward Clopton, with his receipt for the consideration-money, £140, endorsed. It refers to the same piece of land which is described in the preceding article.

131. A counterpart of the deed last mentioned, the original signed by Sir John Clopton, Hugh Clopton, and Thomas Milward, 1702.

132. A shorte and pithie Discourse concerning the engendring, tokens, and effects of all Earthquakes in generall, particularly applyed and conferred with that most strange and terrible worke of the Lord in shaking the Earth, not only within the Citie of London, but also in most partes of all Englande, which hapned vpon Wensday in Easter weeke last past, which was the sixt day of April, almost at sixe a clocke in the euening, in the yeare of our Lord God, 1580. Written by T. T. the 13. of April, 1580. At London, printed by Richarde Iohnes, 1580.—In black-letter with a wood-cut on the title-page. This is the earthquake alluded to by the Nurse in Romeo and Juliet. 4to.

133. An indenture dated 14 May, 3 Elizabeth, between William Clopton of Clopton, co. Warwick,

esquyer, and Thomas Lucy of Charlecote, co. Warwick, esquyer. The latter, afterwards knighted, was the Sir Thomas and Justice Shallow of the great dramatist. With his signature and the seal of the three luces, the whole being in a fine state of preservation, as perfect and bright as when the deed was executed in 1561. The only other specimen, I believe, of his signature accompanied with an impression from the three-luces seal that is in private hands is one in the library of the Marquis of Bath.

134. An original indenture of 1611 with the signature of John Greene, the individual to whom the latest recorded words of Shakespeare were addressed. It is attached as a witness to a legal endorsement of 1612.

135. An original Stratford-on-Avon indenture of 1605, with the signatures of Abraham Sturley and Richard Tyler, the latter having been one of the legatees named in the original draft of the poet's will.

136. An autograph signature of Shakespeare's John a' Combe as a witness to an indenture referring to properties at Stratford-on-Avon, 1593.

137. A fine specimen of the autograph of Thomas Greene, the poet's intimate friend, as a witness to an indenture respecting estates at Old Stratford, Shottery, &c., 1613.

138. An indenture, dated 27 March, 1604, between Sir George Carewe and William Walker, respecting estates in the parish of Stratford-on-Avon, with the signature of Abraham Sturley, the writer of the two letters of 1598 in which there are the curious allusions to Shakespeare.

139. A mortgage indenture of 1564 with the signature of William Clopton, who was the owner of New Place in the middle part of the sixteenth century.

140. The two original indentures of a fine that was levied on New Place between Shakespeare and Underhill in the year 1602. Quite perfect, and in the same condition in which they must have been when in the poet's own hands.

141. An original deed, executed in the year 1605, with the rare autograph, as a witness, of Francis Collyns, who was also one of the witnesses to Shakespeare's will and the poet's solicitor.

142. The original settlement executed on the marriage of Robert Fulwood of Little Alne and Elizabeth, the sister of Richard Hill, rector of Hampton Lucy, 1596. It was witnessed by John Shaxpere, in all probability the poet's father. See an account of this document in Outlines of the Life of Shakespeare, ed. 1886, ii. 246, 247.

143. The original conveyance-deed of New Place from William Clopton of Clopton to William Botte of Stratford-on-Avon, 20 February, 5 Elizabeth, 1563.

144. An indenture made 20 December, 6 Elizabeth, 1563, between William Clopton of Clopton, co. Warwick, esquier, and William Bott of Stratford-on-Avon, relating to the manor of Clopton, " parcell of the premisses cauled the Newe Place," &c.

145. Indentur of certen covenauntes bytwen William Clopton esquyer and Elsabeth Cole, hys syster, for hyr marryage money, 20 July, 24

Henry viii, 1532, charged, inter alia, on "a mesuage or tenemente sett and beyng in Stratford callyd the Newe Place."

146. An Indenture of bargayne and sale of the Newe Place from William Bott and Elizabeth his wife to William Underhill, 1 September, 9 Eliz., 1567. Mutilated. It was from this Underhill that Shakespeare purchased the estate in 1597.

147. An Indenture between Richard Castell of Stratford-on-Avon and Thomas Combe of Old Stratford, to which is attached, on an endorsement dated in 1655, the extremely rare signature of Thomas Combe, the gentleman to whom Shakespeare bequeathed his sword.

148. The original conveyance to Shakespeare of the house in the Blackfriars that he purchased in the year 1613,—made "betweene Henry Walker, citizein and minstrell of London, and William Shakespeare of Stratford-upon-Avon in the Countie of Warwick, gentleman." Quite perfect, and in a beautiful state of preservation. The premises conveyed by this deed were situated within one or two hundred yards to the east of the Blackfriars Theatre. This is the identical record that was enrolled in Chancery, and it has the original official endorsement.

149. The original deed transferring the legal estate of the house last-mentioned, 10 February, 1617-8, in trust to follow the directions of Shakespeare's will, subject only to the remaining term of a lease granted by the poet to one John Robinson. It appears from an endorsement that this deed was handed over at the time to Susanna Hall, the poet's daughter.

150. An original deed of conveyance granted by the Earl of Southampton, Shakespeare's friend and patron, with a fine specimen of his autograph signature. It refers to property at Romsey, near Southampton, and it was executed by the earl in the year 1603, a few weeks after his release from his imprisonment in the Tower of London.

151. An inscribed pane of glass presumed to have been in one of the windows of New Place during the life-time of the poet, but so much deception has been practised in advancing the claims of Shakespearean relics that it is impossible to be too cautious in investigating the testimonies by which those claims are supported. All that is known respecting the present one may thus be briefly stated. It was thus first publicly mentioned in Fairholt's Home of Shakespeare, 1847, p. 27,—"there is an apparently genuine relic of New Place at present (1847) in the possession of the Court family, who own Shakespeare's house. It is a square of glass, measuring nine inches by seven, in which a circular piece is leaded, having the letters W. A. S. for William and Anne Shakespeare, tied in a true lover's knot, and the date, 1615, the year before the poet's death, beneath. A relative of the late Mrs. Court, whose ancestor had been employed to pull down New Place, had saved this square of glass, but attached little value to it. He gave it to her, but she had an honest dislike to the many pretenders to relics, and never showed this glass unless it was expressly requested by the few who had heard of it. She told her story simply, made no comments, and urged no belief. The letters and figures are certainly characteristic; they are painted in dark brown outline, tinted with

yellow; the border is also yellow. The lead is decayed, and the glass loose." The late Mr. Fairholt, one of the best judges in such matters that ever lived, was of a decided opinion that the glass is a genuine work of art of the Shakespearean period. If so, it may be taken for granted that it is an authentic Stratford relic, for it is incredible that any one should have pounced elsewhere upon a glass with the three desirable initials, brought it from a distance into the town, and then invented a New Place story without a commercial or any other sort of intelligible object. But how came the piece of glass to be in the possession of the tenant of the Birth-Place? An explanation has recently presented itself in a passage in a manuscript compiled in the year 1796, and now in the Bodleian (MS. Malone 40); the writer, after mentioning the Clopton painted glass, which, as is well known, was taken by Shakespeare Hart from the Chapel (amongst other refuse from alterations that had been ordered in that building) and inserted in a window of the Birth-Place, says,—"there are several more scraps of painted glass dispersed in other windows of the said premises." Now when New Place was pulled down in the year 1701, Shakespeare Hart was at all events the leading, if not the only, glazier in the town, and it is most likely, if the New Place glass is correctly so designated, that it had been inserted by him in a Birth-Place window, remaining there till 1796, getting afterwards into Mrs. Court's hands through some alteration or repairs in the window in which it had been placed, a more likely hypothesis than her statement as recorded by Fairholt and perhaps misunderstood by him. There is thus somewhat more than a possibility of its genuineness as a

Shakespearean relic, but it is unlikely that evidence leading to a decisive opinion will now ever be accessible. Unless, however, its genuiness as a work of art of the year 1615 be disputed,—and no suspicion in this direction has yet transpired,—even the few known details of its history appear to be explicable only on the assumption that it is a genuine relic of William Shakespeare and Anne Hathaway.

152. An original trust-deed with the signature of Shakespeare Hart, great-grandson of the poet's sister. He spells his name most oddly—*Shaxpeer Hart*—a curious evidence of the local pronunciation of the first name. There are several examples of his signature at Stratford-on-Avon, but this is nearly the only one in private hands.

153. An original deed of 1578, with the extremely rare signature of Shakespeare's schoolmaster, Walter Roche. It relates to a tenement in Ely Street, Stratford-on-Avon.

154. Le Cinqvanta Novelle di Massuccio Salernitano intitolate il Novellino Nvovamente con somma diligentia reviste, corrette, et stampate. Sm. 8vo. Without date or place, but about 1560. —The Shakespeare tale like Romeo and Juliet relates to Mariotto Miguanelli and a girl named Gionozza. See it at p. 239, nov. 33.

155. Two Bookes of Epigrammes and Epitaphs, dedicated to two top-branches of Gentry, Sir Charles Shirley, baronet, and William Davenport esquire. Written by Thomas Bancroft. 4to. Lond. 1639.—The two epigrams on Shakespeare are numbered 118 and 119.

156. The Antiquity and Power of Parliaments in England, written by Mr. Justice Doddridge and several other learned Antiquaries. London, printed for William Leake and John Leake at the Crown in Fleet-street, between the two Temple-Gates, 1679. 12mo.—With a list of books which is curious as showing that Leake had then still on sale his Merchant of Venice of 1652 and his Othello of 1655.

157. Paroemiologia Anglo-Latina, in usum Scholarum concinnata; or Proverbs English and Latine, methodically disposed according to the commonplace heads in Erasmus his Adages, very use-full and delightfull for all sorts of men on all occasions. More especially profitable for Scholars for the attaining Elegancie, sublimitie, and varietie of the best expressions. London, Imprinted by Felix Kyngston for Robert Mylbourne, and are to be sold at the signe of the Vnicorne neere Fleet bridge, 1639. 12mo.—This rare little volume enters into the Shakespearean series by reason of the very curious allusion to the old play of Hamlet at p. 71. The author was master of the free-school at Lincoln.

158. Gli Inganni Comedia del Signor N.S., recitata in Milano l'anno 1547, dinanzi alla Maesta del Re Filippo. Nvovamente ristampata, et con somma diligenza corretta. In Vinegia, 1587. 12mo.—The plot of this comedy resembles that of Twelfth Night.

159. Greene's Groatsworth of Wit bought with a Million of Repentance, describing the Folly of Youth, the falshood of make-shift Flatterers, the Misery of the Negligent, and Mischieves of

deceiving Curtezans. Published at his dying request, and newly corrected, and of many errors purged. London, printed for Henry and Moses Bell, 1637. 4to.—A later edition of the work, originally published in 1592, which contains the singular and first distinct notice of Shakespeare in printed literature.

160. The English Treasury of Wit and Language, collected out of the most and best of our English Drammatick Poems, methodically digested into Common Places for Generall Use. By John Cotgrave, gent. London, printed for Humphrey Moseley, and are to be sold at his Shop at the sign of the Princes Armes in S. Pauls Churchyard, 1655. Small 8vo.—This little volume contains numerous extracts from the works of Shakespeare, some with textual variations.

161. Three Weekes, three daies, and three houres, Observations and Travel from London to Hamborgh in Germanie, amongst Jewes and Gentiles, with Descriptions of Townes and Towers, Castles and Cittadels, artificiall Gallowses, naturall Hangmen; and dedicated for the present to the absent Odcombian knight-errant, Sir Thomas Coriat, Great Brittaines Error and the Worlds Mirror. By Iohn Taylor. London, printed by Edward Griffin, and are to be sold by George Gybbs at the signe of the Flower-deluce in Pauls Churchyard, 1617. 4to.—A curious allusion to the size of "our English Sir Iohn Falstaff" at sig. C.

162. Londinum Florentissma Britanniæ Urbs, emporiumque toto orbe celeberrimum. Visscher excudit.—A long view of London from Whitehall

to Rotherhithe, showing the Globe and the other theatres. This is the second edition of Visscher's celebrated view, undated but published about the year 1625. No other copy known.

163. Abstracts of Title, made about the year 1782, of the house in Chapel Street, Stratford-on-Avon, which belonged in the seventeenth century to the Hathaways, relatives of the poet's wife. They commence with the notice of a feoffment of 8 April, 1647, in which the eastern boundary is given as "the land of Mr. Hall," that is, the garden of New Place.

164. Caius Julius Cæsar Tragædia, ex Plutarcho, Appiano, Alex. Suetonio, D. Cassio, Joh. Xiphilino, &c., maximam partem concinnata, et adversus omnem temerariam seditionem atque tyrannidem ita conscripta, authore M. Casparo Brulovis, Pomerano. Publice exhibita in Academiæ Argentor, theatro, 1616. Small 8vo.

165. An Abstract of Title, 1590 to 1723, of the Fetherstonhaugh London estates. It contains much valuable information respecting Shakespeare's house in the Blackfriars nowhere else to be found, the original deeds, with the exception of one or two, not being known to be in existence.

166. Bond of Susanna Hathaway to Richard Wilson for the performance of covenants, 9 September, 1692. — The original document, with Susanna Hathaway's seal and autograph.

167. Original document respecting the Shakespeares of Lapworth, 1658, signed by Humphrey Shakespeare.

168. Bond of Thomas Hathaway, citizen and joiner of London, for the performance of covenants in an indenture made between Jane Hathaway of Stratford-on-Avon, late wife of Thomas Hathaway, late of Stratford-on-Avon, joiner, deceased, and Thomas Hathaway, son and heir of the said Thomas Hathaway, 14 December, 1662.—The original document, with signature of Thomas Hathaway.

169. A Letter of Attorney of Jane Hathaway of Stratford-upon-Avon, relict of Thomas Hathaway, late of Stratford aforesaid, joyner, deceased, 28 February, 1690–1.—The original document, with the mark and seal of Jane Hathaway.

170. An Indenture respecting the Hathaway house in Chapel Street, Stratford-on-Avon, 14 November, 1662. The original document, but slightly defective.

171. An autograph signature and note of Lord Hunsdon, 1584, the patron of Shakespeare's company in the early years of his theatrical career.

172. An original copy of court-roll in which there are notices of the Shakespeares of Shrewley, co. Warwick, 1605.

173. Il Sacrificio de Gl' Intronati, celebrato ne i Givochi d'vn Carnevale in Siena, et Gl' Ingannati, comedia de i Medesimi. In Venetia, 1554.— 12mo. This is the curious Italian drama the plot of which so greatly resembles that of Twelfth Night. See Hunter's Illustrations of Shakespeare, vol. i., p. 393.

174. Gli Inganni Comedia, dell' illvstriss. Signor Cvrtio Gonzaga. In Venetia, 1592.—This is

the play which is referred to by Manningham in his very curious notice of Twelfth Night, 1602. With engravings of some of the scenes.

175. Jordan's version of Shakespeare's adventure under the crab-tree near Bidford. The original manuscript and the one mentioned in Ireland's Confessions, 1805, p. 34. 8vo.

176. Select Observations on English Bodies, or Cures both Empericall and Historicall performed upon very eminent Persons in desperate Diseases. Written in Latine by Mr. John Hall, physician, living at Stratford-upon-Avon in Warwarickshire. 12mo. Lond. 1657. The first and very rare edition of the cases attended to by Shakespeare's son-in-law.

177. A pleasant and fine Conceited Comedie taken out of the most excellent wittie poet Plautus, chosen purposely from out the rest as least harmefull and yet most delightfull. Written in English by W. W. 4to. Lond. 1595.—There is no evidence that Shakespeare ever saw this production, but Collier may be right in conjecturing that its publication was suggested through the popularity of the Comedy of Errors. Wants the last leaf. Only two other copies known.

178. The Tragedy of Hoffman, or a Reuenge for a Father, as it hath bin diuers times acted with great applause at the Phenix in Druery-lane. London, printed by I. N. for Hugh Perry, and are to bee sold at his shop, at the signe of the Harrow in Brittaines-burse, 1631. — Quarto. "Some degree of resemblance to Hamlet suggests itself both in the general motive of Hoffman and in the madness of the heroine,"

Ward's History of English Dramatic Literature, vol. i., p. 232.

179. An Æthiopian Historie written in Greeke by Heliodorus, very wittie and pleasaunt. Englished by Thomas Underdoune. Imprinted at London by Henrie Wykes for Fraunces Coldocke, dwellinge in Powles Churche-yarde at the signe of the Greene Dragon.—Quarto. An edition of extreme rarity. A story in this work is alluded to in Twelfth Night, v. 1.

180. The Famous Tragedy of the Rich Iew of Malta, as it was played before the King and Queene in his Majesties Theatre at White-Hall by her Majesties Servants at the Cock-pit. Written by Christopher Marlo. London, printed by I. B. for Nicholas Vavasour, and are to be sold at his Shop in the Inner Temple neere the Church 1633.—Quarto. There cannot be much doubt that Shakespeare had either witnessed a representation of, or acted in, this tragedy at the Rose Theatre. No earlier edition known.

181. The story of the drunkard, similar to that which is dramatized in the Induction to the Taming of the Shrew, from Barckley's Discovrse of the Felicitie of Man, 1598.

182. A manuscript list of the common fields in Snitterfield, 1765, as they existed previously to the enclosure. Useful for the identification of the Shakespearean properties. Quarto.

183. A pleasant Comedie of Faire Em, the Millers Daughter of Manchester, with the Loue of William the Conqueror. As it was sundry times publiquely acted in the Honourable Citie of Lon-

don, by the right Honourable the Lord Strange his Seruants. London, printed for Iohn Wright, and are to be sold at his shop at the signe of the Bible in Guilt-spur street without New-gate, 1631. Quarto.

184. A Woman is a Weather-cocke, a new Comedy, as it was acted before the King in White-Hall, and diuers times Priuately at the White-Friers by the Children of her Maiesties Reuels. Written by Nat: Field. Printed at London for Iohn Budge, and are to be sold at the great South doore of Paules, and at Brittaines Bursse, 1612.— Quarto. Field was one of Shakespeare's most eminent colleagues.

185. An Heptameron of Ciuill Discourses, containing the Christmasse Exercise of sundrie well Courted 'Gentlemen and Gentlewomen, &c. A worke intercoursed with Ciuyll Pleasure to reaue tediousnesse from the Reader, and garnished with Morall Noates to make it profitable to the Regarder. The Reporte of George Whetstone, gent. At London, printed by Richard Iones, at the signe of the Rose and Crowne neare Holburne Bridge, 3 Feb. 1582.—Quarto. This rare volume includes the foundation-story of Measure for Measure.

186. A most pleasant Comedy of Mucedorus, the King's Son of Valentia, and Amadine, the King's Daughter of Aragon. With the merry Conceits of Mouse. 4to. Lond. 1668.

187. The Waking Mans Dreame, from the Admirable Events of John Peter Camus, 4to. Lond. 1639.—This is the Story of the Induction to the Taming of the Shrew.

188. The Anatomy of the English Nvnnery at Lisbon in Portvgall, dissected and laid open by one that was some-time a yonger Brother of the Covent. 4to. Lond. 1622.—The curious notice of Shakespeare's Venus and Adonis will be found at p. 17.

189. Remaines concerning Britaine, but especially England and the Inhabitants thereof. Reviewed, corrected, and encreased. Printed at London by Iohn Legatt for Simon Waterson, 1614.—In this edition there was first printed the tract on the Excellencie of the English Tongue that includes the curious notice of Shakespeare.

190. The White Divel, or the Tragedy of Paulo Giordano Vrsini, Duke of Brachiano, with the Life and Death of Vittoria Corombona, the famous Venetian Curtizan. Acted by the Queenes Maiesties Seruants. Written by Iohn Webster. London, printed by N. O. for Thomas Archer, and are to be sold at his Shop in Popes Head Pallace, neere the Royall Exchange, 1612.—Quarto. An allusion to Shakespeare in the address to the reader.

191. The Philosophers Satyrs, written by M. Robert Anton of Magdalen Colledge in Cambridge. London, printed by T. C. and B. A. for Roger Iackson, and are to be sold at his shop in Fleet-street, ouer against the great Conduit, 1616.—Quarto. The earliest work in which there is an allusion to Shakespeare's tragedy of Antony and Cleopatra.

192. A Collection of Poems, being all the Miscellanies of Mr. William Shakespeare. London, printed for Bernard Lintott. This edition was published in 1709. An interesting and unique copy,

with Dr. Farmer's manuscript notes, collations, and cuttings from contemporary newspapers. In a preliminary note is the curious account of the letter said to have been written to Shakespeare by James I.

193. M. William Shake-speare, his True Chronicle History of the Life and Death of King Lear and his Three Daughters. With the Vnfortunat Life of Edgar and his sullen assumed humour of Tom of Bedlam. As it was plaid before the Kings Maiesty at Whit-Hall vpon S. Stephens night in Christmas Hollidaies. By his Maiesties Servants, playing vsually at the Globe on the Bank-side. London, printed by Jane Bell, and are to be sold at the East-end of Christ-Church, 1655.—Quarto.

194. An indenture, 20 February, 18 James I., 1621, between the Urles and Sandells of Shottery, one of the latter being Fulke, the son, I believe, of Shakespeare's marriage-bondsman. Witnessed, amongst others, by Edmund Hathaway, a marksman.

195. A conveyance of 9 September, 1692, from Susanna Hathaway, spinster, grand-daughter of Thomas Hathaway, heretofore of Stratford-on-Avon, joiner, to Richard Wilson of St. Giles's, Cripplegate, of the house in Chapel Street that belonged to the relatives of Shakespeare's Anne Hathaway. The original, with the vendor's signature. The "land now or heretofore of Mr. Hall," that is, the New Place Great Garden, is mentioned as one of the boundaries.

196. A black-letter fragment of the Hundred Mery Talys, a book of stories mentioned by

Shakespeare. It is part only of the curious anecdote of John-a-Droyns.

197. A copy of verses by R. P. Jodrell on the mulberry-tree planted by Shakespeare and cut down by the Rev. Francis Gastrell.

198. The original certificate from the Justices of the Peace of Middlesex respecting the Blackfriars Theatre, 20 November, 1633, a report on the value of the property, its tenure by the Burbages, &c. This interesting document, first noticed in Collier's New Facts, 1835, p. 27, has been pronounced a forgery without the shadow of a reason. It is, in my opinion, of unquestionable authenticity, and I will back that opinion with the observation that, should the officials of the British Museum and our national Record office collectively arrive at a different conclusion, I will cheerfully give fifty guineas to the funds of any charity that they may do me the favour to indicate.

199. A terier of the halfe yard land at Shottery which Giles Roberts houlds of John Hatheway, May, 1647.

200. Counterpart lease, 27 May, 1647, of land at Shottery, from John Hathaway, yeoman, and Elizabeth his wife, to Giles Roberts of Luddington.

201. Shakespearean scraps from original copies of the following works.—Decker's Satiro-Mastix, 1602; list of books sold by Ga. Bedell and Th. Collins, 1656; Brathwait's Strappado for the Divell, 1615; Sheppard's Epigrams, 1651; Marston's Parasitaster, 1606; Cranley's Converted Courtezan, 1639; the Returne from Pernassus, 1606; Brome's Joviall Crew, 1652; A Helpe to

E

Discourse, 1640; Letters of Sir Tobie Mathews, 1660; Swan's Speculum Mundi, 1643; The Hogge hath lost his Pearle, 1614; the Palace of Pleasure; Eastward Hoe, 1605; Every Man out of his Humour, 1600; Nash's Pierce Penilesse; Whetstone's Heptameron, 1582; Ben Jonson's Execration against Vulcan, 1640; Decker's Dead Terme, 1608.

202. Autograph letter of Thomas Warton, 1770, respecting the Wilmecote Shakespearean traditions.

203. Administration of the Effects of Robert Hathaway, late of Shottery in the parish of Old Stratford, granted to his widow Sarah in 1728.

204. Probate copy, with an annexed memorandum, 1692, of the will of Richard Hathaway of Shottery, in the parish of Old Stratford, yeoman, 26 November, 1684.

205. A deed of 1692 in which three members of the same family, a London stationer, his uncle and mother, have written their surnames on the same day in three various orthographies.

206. Facsimiles of extracts from the Henley Street deeds, 1611 to 1639; of the entry respecting the funeral of Shakespeare's daughter Anne; of manuscript notes from a copy of the Second Part of Henry the Fourth, 1600; of the mark-signature of Joseph Phillips of the Falcon tavern, Stratford-on-Avon; and of Quiney's letter to Shakespeare, October, 1598.

207. A bond for the performance of covenants, with the signatures of Shakespeare Hart and William Shakespeare Hart, 1727.

208. A facsimile tracing, beautifully executed by E. W. Ashbee, of the conveyance-deed of Shakespeare's Blackfriars estate, 1613.

209. The music to the song of "My flocks feed not," from the madrigals of Thomas Weelkes, 1597; a version of one of the poems introduced into the Passionate Pilgrim.

210. Two facsimiles of extracts respecting Shakespeare the shoemaker, 1589, 1592; Where the bee sucks, from the Musical Companion, 1672; facsimile of attestation to a Henley Street deed of 1573; memorandum in the autograph of R. B. Wheler respecting Anne Hathaway's cottage; two Shakespearean scraps from the Workes of Ben Jonson, ed. 1616.

211. Original title-page of the Puritaine or the Widdow of Watling-streete, 1607; autograph of Jonson on the fly-leaf of an edition of Martial, 1619, one of Ben's favourite authors; title and preface to Shakespeare's Poems, 1640; notice of Shakespeare from the last leaf of Heywood's Apology for Actors, 1612.

212. A plan of Oxford, c. 1640.

213. A deed respecting the Hathaway house in Chapel Street, Stratford-on-Avon, 20 March, 1696. The New Place boundary mentioned. Signed by Susanna Hathaway.

214. An indenture, 30 April, 8 James I., 1610, respecting land at Shottery. Witnessed by Francis Collins, the poet's friend and solicitor.—Another indenture, 10 October, 1605, with two finer examples of Collins's signature.

215. A Mappe of Penbrokeshire, Glamorganshire, Monmouthshire, Glostershire, Somersetshire, Dorsetshire, Devonshire, and Cornwall, part of Wiltshire, etc. An edition of Hollar's map of 1644, with the roads inserted by a later hand, the earliest, I believe, in which there is a delineation of the road to Barnstaple, a town visited by Shakespeare's company in 1605.

216. An early, perhaps the earliest, title-page in which a quotation from Shakespeare is introduced, that of Pendragon or the Carpet Knight his Kalendar, 1698; a biographical notice of Shakespeare from an Historical Dictionary of England and Wales, 1692; Shakespearean scraps from Harington's Ariosto, 1591, and Davenant's Works, 1673; the dimensions of Stratford-on-Avon Church, a paper by the Rev. Joseph Greene, c. 1762; Shakespearean notices in a list of books printed for Thomas Bennet, 1697, and in the induction to Bartholomew Fair.

217. An attestation from a deed of the year 1555, relating to a messuage in the village of Packwood, co. Warwick, one Christofer Shaxspere being one of the witnesses.

218. A deed of 1647 respecting the Hathaway house in Chapel Street, Stratford-on-Avon. The original indenture signed by the Lanes.

219. The engraved portrait of Shakespeare by Droeshout on a copy of the title-page of the second folio edition of the poet's works, 1632. This is one of the only four impressions known of the title-page of the edition of 1632 before the spelling of the word *coppies* was altered, a circumstance which, although apparently trivial, is of value as

showing that it includes one of the earliest impressions from the plate after it had been used for the first folio.

220. The engraved head of Shakespeare on the title-page of the first collective edition of his plays, 1623, Martin Droeshout sculpsit, London. The original engraving by Droeshout before it was altered by an inferior hand; of extreme rarity, and the earliest engraved portrait of Shakespeare in existence.

The following observations upon this proof-engraving are from the pen of the late F. W. Fairholt, F.S.A.,—" the portrait in this state of the engraving is remarkable for clearness of tone; the shadows being very delicately rendered, so that the light falls upon the muscles of the face with a softness not to be found in the ordinary impressions. This is particularly visible in the arch under the eye, and in the muscles of the mouth; the expression of the latter is much altered in the later states of the plate by the enlargement of the upturned moustache, which hides and destroys the true character of this part of the face. The whole of the shadows have been darkened by cross-hatching and coarse dotting, particularly on the chin; this gives a coarse and undue prominence to some parts of the portrait, the forehead particularly. In this early state of the plate the hair is darker than any of the shadows on the head, and flows softly and naturally; in the retouched plate the shadow is much darker than the roots of the hair, imparting a swelled look to the head and giving the hair the appearance of a raised wig. It is remarkable that no shadow falls across the collar; this omission, and the general low tone of colour in the engraving, may have induced the retouching and strengthening which has injured the true character of the likeness, which, in its original state, is far more worthy of Ben Jonson's commendatory lines."—The late Mr. William Smith, Director of the National Portrait Gallery, whose knowledge of early engraving was unrivalled, thus wrote to me in reference to a suggestion that the variations were caused by an accident to the plate,—" I was unwilling to answer your note until I had made another careful examination of your engraving, as well as of the very fine impression in the usual state which we have recently purchased for the National Portrait Gallery. This I have now done, and I can find no traces of any damage whatever. I fully believe that, on what is technically termed proving the plate, it was thought that much of the work was so delicate as not to allow of a sufficient number of impressions being printed. Droeshout might probably have refused to spoil his work, and it was retouched by an inferior and coarser engraver."

221. A rough ground-plan on vellum of the College at Stratford-on-Avon, with the adjoining roads, made very early in the sixteenth century. The site of the *tyth barne* is shown. This is by far the earliest plan of any part of the town that is known to exist.

222. A presentment made att a leete there (Stretford Burgus) holden the vij.° daye of Aprill, anno xxxiij.° Elizabeth regine, 1591. This very curious perambulation of the borough of Stratford is quoted in the sixth chapter of Knight's Biography of Shakspere as being then, 1843, in the possession of Mr. R. B. Wheler, but there is a mistake in

thinking that the old boundary elm, a sketch of which is given in that work and which was cut down in 1847, was the identical tree mentioned in the present document. It stood, however, on the same site, that is to say, on the bank between the turnpike road and the foot-path to Birmingham, just beyond the lane to Clopton.

223. A grant from James de Clopton to Walter de Cokefeld of a messuage and lands at Clopton and in la Grave. A deed of the time of Henry III. One of the witnesses is noted as Richard de Peyto, showing at how early a period the surname of Peto was known in the neighbourhood of Stratford-on-Avon.

224. A grant from Peter de Montefort to Isabel, daughter of Stephen Norton, clericus, and Edmund de Middeltone, her son, of a messuage and lands within the manor of Clopton, temp. Hen. III. The boundaries, which are given with unusual minuteness, including notices (with the names) of upwards of thirty fields or common-lands, go far to prove, in conjunction with the memorandum of 1614 respecting Shakespeare's outlying property, that the poet held nothing at Clopton.

225. A lease with the autograph of Richard Hyll, the woollen-draper, penned a few months before his death in 1593. This individual, whose singular metrical epitaph is yet to be seen in Stratford Church, was intimately acquainted with the poet's family, having been bail for his father in some law proceedings that were instituted against him in 1587.

226. A lease for twenty-one years, dated 22 November, 1562, from William Clopton of Clopton,

esquire, to William Smythe of Stratford-on-Avon, haberdasher, of a close of land "in the lordshyp of Cloptone, beneythe the park next unto the coman fyldes ther, now in the tenure and occupacyon of the said William Smyth." The consideration paid for the lease was £31, the reserved annual rent being "only on cowple of capons." Witnessed by William Bott, the purchaser of New Place. Signed by William Smythe, the deed itself being in the autograph of Henry Higford, the steward of the Stratford Court of Record. This latter circumstance invests the document with no little degree of interest, the accounts drawn up by the poet's father in 1564 and 1565 being in the same handwriting. It is also worth notice that John Shakespeare acted as one of the Chamberlains when William Smythe nominally held the office in the year last-mentioned.

227. A lease from Sir George and Lady Carewe, 27 March, 2 James I., 1604. to William Courte of Stratford-on-Avon, gentleman, of land near the Wier Brake. With the signature of William Courte, who was one of Shakespeare's neighbours in Chapel Street and concerned with others in the tithe-suit that was instituted by the poet about the year 1609.

228. Another lease from the same, 27 March, 1604, to John Lane of Stratford-on-Avon, gentleman, of "all that close called Crosse on the Hill," &c. Witnessed, with their autographs, by the William Courte, mentioned in the preceding article, and by Abraham Sturley, the individual who was interesting himself in the poet's investments in the year 1598.

229. A play-bill of the time of William the Third, announcing a performance of Dryden's Troilus and Cressida on October the 28th, 1697. This is the earliest authentic play-bill of a Shakespearean character which is known to exist. Play-bills, or "billes for players," as they are termed in the Stationers' Registers for 1587, were in ordinary use throughout the time of the great dramatist, but none earlier than the reign of William the Third are known to be in existence. Even any of the latter are of extreme rarity. The names of actors do not appear to have been inserted before the time of George the Second, the frequently-quoted bill of the Humorous Lieutenant, 1663, being an undoubted forgery.

230. Shakespearean scraps from original copies of the following works,—Drayton's Elegies, 1631; Randolph's Hey for Honesty, 1651; a Declaration of the Treasons of the Earl of Essex, 1601; Kirkman's list, 1671; Blurt Master Constable, 1602; Goulart's Histories of our Time, 1607; Suckling's Fragmenta Aurea, 1648; Cokain's Small Poems of Divers Sorts, 1658; Sharpe's Noble Stranger, 1640; Marston's Malcontent, 1604; Cawdray's Treasurie or Store-house of Similies, 1600; Sir Thomas Smithes Voiage and Entertainment in Rushia, 1605; the Palace of Pleasure; Playford's Musical Companion, 1667; Scarron's Comical Romance or Facetious History, 1676; Cartwright's Poems, 1651.

231. Itinerant players acting on a scaffold in what is generally said to be a view of Old Smithfield. An engraving from Scarron's Comical Romance, 1676, "printed for W. Crooke at the Green Dragon without Temple Barr."

232. A plan of the city of Bath. Speed, 1610.

233. Four pages from a prompter's copy, temp. Car. II., of the tragedy of Macbeth, with numerous alterations of the original text.

234. The title-page of the second folio edition of Shakespeare's Plays, 1632, with the Droeshout portrait. This copy differs from that in No. 219, the word *copies* being rightly spelt and the notice "at his shop" being omitted in the imprint.

235. Two copies of the Droeshout portrait from the early folios, but from which editions is unknown. The first came to my hands in an illustrated copy of the octavo variorum, the compiler of which had reduced the width of the engraving by a barbarian clipping of the sides.

236. Paul's Cross, a wood-engraving in the title-page of Three Looks over London, 1643.

237. A woodcut facsimile of Shakespeare's Rime he made at the Myter in Fleete Streete, from a manuscript compiled about the year 1640.

238. The View of London Bridge from East to West,—to the Right Honorable Sir Ric. Salstonstall, Lord Mayor of the Cittie of London. He was mayor in 1597, the obvious date of this undated engraving, which is slightly pared on the lower margin. An inferior variation of it was published in 1624, but no other copy in this first state is known to exist. Mr. William Rendle, the historian of Southwark, thus writes respecting this engraving in Notes and Queries of June the 5th, 1886—"now visiting my friend Mr. Halliwell-Phillipps, I have been favoured by him with the sight of a large plate, Norden's London Bridge, in his possession,

as beautiful as it is rare. The ordinary copy, in its main features like this one, is so different in some other respects that I am tempted to send you the particulars. I suppose it to be the one referred to in the 1624 print thus. 'I described it in the time of Queene Elizabeth, but the plate having bene neare these twenty yeares imbezeled and detained by a person, till of late unknown, and now brought to light,' &c. From its clearness and sharpness, it must be one of the earliest, if not the earliest, impression, and from the writing on it, so exactly like Norden's, probably his own copy. Cropped at the bottom it yet shows its date by the dedication to the 'Right Honorable Sr Ric' Saltonstall, Lord May^r of the Citti of London,' as 1597, as the ordinary copy dedicated to Sir John Gore implies 1624.—We face the eastern side of the bridge, and looking through the arches, see the Bankside with its continuous houses. As in the later print, boats are upset and people are struggling in the water, but in this the features and costume of the many more people in many more boats are very clear; there are boats sharp at both ends, sharp at one end, boats with one or two persons, one with five. Midstream are four wide, large, rounded boats, empty, one covered with a sort of caged work, possibly, I think, bumboats or for conveyance of goods generally, the caged one perhaps for lively cattle, or it may be for the securing pressed men for the tenders at the Tower close at hand.—The arms of the earlier print have the lion one side, a dragon the other, with, underneath, 'Semper eadem'; in the 1624 copy the dragon gives place to the unicorn, and the 'Semper eadem' to 'Dieu et mon droit.' The writing is as follows:—At the top, 'Pontis Londinensis facies orientalis,

Joanne Norden descriptore.' South end, where the 'Bear-at-the-Bridge-foot' was, 'Southewark-Bridge-gate.' Immediately over the heads on poles, 'the Draw-bridge.' By Nonsuch, 'Capella S. Thomæ'; further on 'S. Marie Lock. Newe fish street.' Then 'Longitudo hujus Pontis est prope 800 pedes. Altitudo est 60 ped. Latitudo est 30 pedes. Domus institorum et mercatorum, hic qui omnis generis merces vendunt. Sunt supra 100, &c." This is the earliest separate large view of the bridge known to exist, and there is no other that can be confidently assigned to the period of Elizabeth.

239. Braun's plan of London, 1574, uncoloured and in an earlier state than the copy No. 313.

240. Profil de la Ville de Londre, cappitalle dv Royavme Dangleterre. Undated, but published, I believe, at Paris in 1641. This long view includes the Swan and Globe Theatres, and was therefore taken from a much earlier one.

241. The engraved title-page to Sir Richard Baker's Chronicle of the Kings of England, 1643, including a miniature view of London and Southwark that exhibits two of the Bankside theatres.

242. A plan of Westminster, London and Southwarke, W. Hollar fecit. Dedicated to Sir Robert Vynar by Richard Blome, 1673.

243. The Kingdome of Great Britaine and Ireland, graven by I. Hondius, and are to be solde by I. Sudbury and George Humble in Popes Head Alley in London, 1610. With a view of London showing the old Globe Theatre in the foreground. Coloured.

244. Londinum Celeberrimum Angliæ Emporium, published at Amsterdam by Dancker Danckerts, 1640. A view of London showing the Swan, the Bear Garden, and the Globe.

245. Proceedings "att a Session of the Sewers holden in Southwark," July and October, 1653, respecting the one " in Maide Lane nere the place where the Globe playhouse lately stood." This interesting document establishes the exact locality of the theatre.

246. Original documents in which there are references to the Shakespeares of Kingswood, a hamlet of Lapworth, 1658–1673. The earliest of them has the autograph of Humphrey Shakespeare, considered by Malone, ed. 1821, ii. 62, to have been the son of John, the shoemaker of Stratford. —An indenture relating to land at Packwood, co. Warwick, 1528, in which there is a notice of Cristofer Shakspeyre.

247. An indenture respecting the Falcon in Southwark, 11 April, 32 Hen. VIII., 1541, a tavern said, but on very uncertain grounds, to have been frequented by Shakespeare.

248. A levie and taxacion for the reliefe of the poore in the parishe of Old Stratford, in the countie of Warwicke, by the churchwardens and overseers for the poore there, whose names are heervnder written the xiij.th daie of Aprill, 1640, with the mark-signature of John Hathaway.—A levie made the tenthe daie of August, 1635, by Roger Barnard and Thomas Harris, churchwardens of the parish of Old Stratford, towardes the repaire of the Parishe Church there, with autograph of Edmund Hathaway.—These two manuscripts, which contain

several entries of Shakespearean interest, were amongst those which were lately discovered by Mr. Sims of the British Museum in the archives of Wallop Hall, co. Salop.

249. A document on vellum respecting lands in Kent leased to Sir Robert Sidney, with the signature of Robert, Earl of Essex, 1596.—There can scarcely be a doubt that this nobleman, the object of the graceful compliment in Henry the Fifth, was on friendly terms with the great dramatist.

250. A deed of covenant, 10 October, 1647, for the levy of a fine on the land where the Bear in Bridge Street, Stratford-on-Avon, formerly stood, and on the house in Chapel Street that had been purchased by Thomas Hathaway, a lineal descendant from the parents of Shakespeare's wife.

251. A deed with the mark-signature of John Richardson of Shottery, 1610, the son perhaps of one of Shakespeare's marriage-bondsmen.—A levy made by the inhabitants of Lapworth, 1650, including notices of the Shakespeares of that parish. —Shakespearean scraps from an original copy of Gayton's Pleasant Notes upon Don Quixot, 1654.

252. John Jones and Mary his wife, the widow and relict of John Hathaway, to Robert Hathaway of Shottery, a receipt for a legacy bequeathed to Mary by her first husband, 6 August, 1703.

253. A collection of Shakespearean scraps from Camden's Remaines, 1605 to 1636.

254. An inventory of the goods and chatels of Robert Hathaway (here spelt Athaway) of Shotrey, in the parish of Old Stratford, lately deceased,

1728. An important document. See Outlines of the Life of Shakespeare, ed. 1887, ii. 192.

255. Deed of gift of personal effects from Sarah Hathaway, widow of Robert Hathaway of Shottery, to Susannah Taylor, her daughter, wife of William Taylor, 1752.

256. An indenture and bond, March, 1604, respecting land near Stratford-on-Avon, with two signatures of Richard Tyler, a contemplated legatee under Shakespeare's will. The bond is witnessed by Abraham Sturley, the person who interested himself in the poet's business arrangements of 1598.

257. Facsimile of an entry respecting Sir Thomas Lucy, 1595; manuscript notes by R. B. Wheler on the Charlecote traditions; a fragment from the Rev. Joseph Greene's revised copy of Rowe's Life of Shakespeare, the portion referring to the Charlecote adventure, c. 1750; facsimiles of the signatures and attestation to the poet's will, Neele sculpsit; the second nominated allusion to Shakespeare in our printed literature, the original leaves from Polimanteia, 1595.

258. An original deed with the rare signature of *the* Sir Thomas Lucy of Charlecote, the individual who owes his celebrity to his inconsiderate treatment of the youth who was afterwards to be the national dramatist of England. This indenture was executed in December, 17 Elizabeth, 1574, and it bears also the signatures of Sir Thomas's two brothers, Timothy and Edward.

259. The conveyance of a piece of land, 20 April, 14 James I., 1616, from Sir Thomas Lucy

of Charlcott, in the county of Warwick, knight, to James Combe of Hyneleadon, in the county of the cittye of Glocester, yoman, with the signature of the former. This Sir Thomas was fond of literary society, but there is no good evidence in favour of the oft-repeated assertion that he was on friendly terms with the great dramatist. He was the grandson of the poet's Justice Shallow, who, as well as the intermediate Sir Thomas Lucy, is mentioned in the present indenture.

260. Memoranda in the autograph of Philip, Earl of Pembroke and Montgomery. They are of great curiosity, including four notices of one "Squeal of Cotswold," who appears to have been a very indifferent character; singular evidences of the poet's introducing the name of a local celebrity of his own day into an historical drama.

261. A large plan of the basement of a house adjoining northwards to New Place.

262. Indenture, 14 June, 12 Elizabeth, 1570, respecting lands at Snitterfield and Fulbrooke, with a signature of Bartholomew Hales. Witnessed amongst others by Thomas Perkes and Alexander Webbe, the poet's uncle.

263. A Plan of the Town and Borough of Stratford-upon-Avon by W. R. Swanwick. Engraved by J. Tolley, Birmingham. Published by J. Ward, Stratford.

264. Indenture of lease, 10 November, 17 James I., 1619, of a piece of land called Little Rushbrooke, situated at Bridgetown, Stratford-on-Avon, with the signatures of Lord and Lady Carew of Clopton, a traditional anecdote respecting whom is believed

to have been in the poet's thoughts when he makes Prospero speak so enigmatically of the loss of his daughter.

265. A very large plan of Stratford-on-Avon, divided into four sheets, executed about the year 1780. It should be noticed that some of the memoranda are of a more recent date than that of the drawing itself.

266. A view of the interior of the chancel of Stratford Church, published at Birmingham in December, 1827. Drawn by H. Hutchinson; engraved by W. Radclyffe. Two copies, one of them in the rare state before the insertion of the carved roof.

267. Ancient bedroom in George's farm-house at Grendon Underwood; Elizabethan houses at Aylesbury. Two sketches taken by Blight in September, 1865.

268. Charlecote House, river front. Drawn by J. V. Barber. Engraved by W. Radclyffe. Published at Birmingham, September, 1824.

269. Charlecote House and Gateway, front view. Drawn by J. D. Harding. Engraved by W. Radclyffe. Published at Birmingham, March, 1827.

270. Tracings of the inscriptions under Shakespeare's monumental effigy and on his tomb-stone, taken by Mr. William Butcher, jun., in 1885; with a rubbing of the former.

271. A water-colour sketch of the exterior of Stratford Church, executed about the year 1840.

F

272. The monumental effigy, engraved by I. S. Agar from an original drawing by A. Wivell in the possession of John Cordy, esq. Published by Geo. Lawford, November, 1825. A proof.

273. Shakespearean scraps from an original copy of Burton's Anatomy of Melancholy, 1628.

274. An Account of the English Dramatick Poets, or Some Observations and Remarks on the Lives and Writings of all those that have publish'd Comedies, &c. By Gerard Langbaine. Oxford, 1691.—Octavo. With a few manuscript notes by Oldys. Account of Shakespeare at pp. 453–469.

275. A Brief Account of Stratford-upon-Avon, with a particular Description and Survey of the Collegiate Church, the Mausoleum of Shakespeare. 12mo. Stratford, printed by E. Walford, n.d. This, which is the earliest guide-book to Stratford, was published about the year 1791.

276. An account of the discovery of John Shakespeare's Confession of Faith, with notes on other Shakespearean traditions, by John Jordan, 1790. Folio. Autograph manuscript.

277. A volume of miscellaneous poems, many of which are quaint and curious, collected, apparently by an Oxford student, chiefly between the years 1633 and 1639. This interesting manuscript includes, at ff. 12.b, 26, two of Shakespeare's sonnets, the seventy-first and thirty-second. Also, at f. 20, "Take, oh take, those lipps awaie," with additional verses. Allusions to Pericles and Julius Cæsar, the latter termed "the tragœdy of Brutus and Cassius," at f. 62. "On the Earle of Penbrookes death, or Earle uppon Earle," f. 85.

278. A manuscript collection of verses and epitaphs made in the time of Pope. It includes, at p. 2, the verses on John-a-Combe, here stated to be "by Shakespear." 4to.

279. Essayes of Certaine Paradoxes. The second Impression, inlarged. London, printed for Richard Hawkins, and are to be sold at his Shop neare Serjeants-Inne in Chancery-Lane, 1617. Quarto.—The allusions to the Richard the Third plays will be found at sigs. C. 3 and E. 3.

280. A Bright Burning Beacon forewarning all wise Virgins to trim their lampes against the comming of the Bridegroome, conteining a generall doctrine of sundrie signes and wonders, specially earthquakes both particular and generall; a discourse of the end of this world; a commemoration of our late Earthquake the 6. of April, about 6. of the clocke in the euening, 1580. Newly translated and collected by Abraham Fleming. Imprinted at London by Henrie Denham, dwelling in Paternoster Rowe at the signe of the Starre.—12mo. This is the earthquake which is alluded to in Romeo and Juliet.

281. A Godly Exhortation by occasion of the late iudgement of God shewed at Parris-Garden the thirteenth day of Ianuarie, where were assembled by estimation aboue a thousand persons, whereof some were slaine, and of that number, at the least, as is crediblie reported, the thirde person maimed and hurt. Giuen to all estates for their instruction concerning the keeping of the Sabboth day. By John Field, minister of the word of God. 12mo. At London, printed by Robert Walde-grave, dwelling without Temple-barre, for Henry Carre in Paules Churchyard, 1583.

282. An extract from Rowe's Life of Shakespeare, revised by the Rev. Joseph Greene of Stratford-on-Avon about the year 1750. Exceedingly important in the question of the identification of the Hathaway cottage at Shottery. 8vo. Manuscript.

283. England's Parnassus, or the choysest Flowers of our Moderne Poets, with their Poeticall Comparisons. Descriptions of Bewties, Personages, Castles, Pallaces, Mountaines, Groues, Seas, Springs, Riuers, &c. Whereunto are annexed other various discourses, both pleasaunt and profitable. Imprinted at London for N.L., C.B., and T.H. 1600.—Small octavo. An interesting collection that includes numerous extracts from the works of Shakespeare. This copy, which belonged successively to Theobald and Oldys, is perhaps unique in one small matter, the two fly-leaves of sheet A preceding the title-page. In common with two other copies in the British Museum, it has not the verses commencing, "Fame's windy trump," which have been said, I am sure erroneously, to form a genuine portion of the work.

284. Mount Tabor, or Private Exercises of a Penitent Sinner, serving for a daily Practice of the life of Faith, &c., written in the time of a voluntary retrait from secular affaires. By R. W. esquire. Published in the yeare of his age 75, anno Dom. 1639.—Some of the "exercises" of this author, who was born in the same year with Shakespeare, are strikingly illustrative of the boy and school life of exactly the poet's own time. At p. 110 is the well-known chapter "upon a stage-play which I saw when I was a child."

285. Playes Confuted in fiue Actions, prouing that they are not to be suffred in a Christian common weale; by the waye both the Cauils of Thomas Lodge and the Play of Playes written in their defence, and other objections of Players frendes, are truely set downe and directlye aunsweared. By Steph. Gosson, Stud. Oxon. London, imprinted for Thomas Gosson, dwelling in Paternoster Row at the signe of the Sunne, n.d.—12mo. The original black-letter edition.

286. Original sketches taken by J. P. Neale in 1825 of parts of the Church of the Holy Trinity, Stratford-on-Avon, with others of the font and the base of the market-cross, the two latter relics then in the possession of Captain Saunders.

287. A fragment of an original contemporary manuscript of Marlowe's Massacre of Paris, containing a number of passages that were omitted in the old printed edition. This interesting relic, which was first noticed in Collier's History of Dramatic Poetry, 1831, iii. 133, is the only vestige of the tragedy in the state in which it left the hands of the author, and is important as a striking evidence of the extent to which texts of some of our early dramas were mutilated in the copies that were used by the printers.

288. An impression of Droeshout's engraved portrait of Shakespeare, issued by Henry Herringman and Thomas Dring in the year 1673. No other copy known.

289. Births, marriages, and burials of the Shakespear family, faithfully transcrib'd from the register-book of the parish of Stratford-on-Avon, with a note respecting the Hathaway house at

Shottery, by the Rev. Joseph Greene, 1769–1770. The accuracy of the extracts from the register is certified by the Rev. Stephen Nason, the then vicar. 4to.

290. The Last Judgment, or the Day of Doom, copied by Fisher in 1804 from paintings discovered on the west side of the wall that divides the nave and chancel of the Guild Chapel. —Miracles of the Holy Cross, two paintings on the north side of the Chancel, Fisher del. The original drawings, coloured, and, like the other ones by the same artist in this collection, more accurate than the published reproductions. They are now unique, the only replicas that were made having perished with the rest of the Staunton library.

291. The tombs of Sir Thomas Lucy (the poet's Justice Shallow) and his son, from the monuments in Charlecote Church. W. Hollar fecit, 1656.

292. The Arches of Triumph erected in honour of King James the First at his Majesties entrance and passage through his honourable Citty of London, upon the 15th day of March, 1603-4. Five of the original very rare contemporary engravings by William Kip, Stephen Harrison, and another, including the one which has the view of London. There is authentic record evidence that Shakespeare was in the procession on this interesting occasion.

293. Thomas Lucie, miles, the grandson of the poet's Sir Thomas, a monument on the south side of the chancel in Charlecote Church. P. Lombart sculpsit Londini, 1656.

294. A plan of Shrewsbury, from Speed's Theatre of Great Britaine, 1610.

295. The monumental effigy of Shakespeare with the verses underneath and those on the grave-stone. Dugdale, 1656.

296. Exterior of Stratford Church. An uncoloured lithograph by J. Salmon, from a drawing by Mrs. Dighton. Published at Stratford-on-Avon, 1835.

297. A south-east view of the exterior of Stratford Church. A large original drawing in water-colours by J. C. Buckler, 1823.

298. A large pen-and-ink drawing of the exterior of Stratford Church, showing the tower and southern side of the western end, executed about the year 1762. This and the next-mentioned drawing were in Richard Greene's illustrated copy of Dugdale, but it may be suspected, from the style, that they were not executed by him.

299. A Mappe of Kent, Sovthsex, Surrey, Middlesex, Barke and Southamptonshire and the Ile of Vight, and part of Essex and Wiltshire, etc. W. Hollar, 1644. See No. 308.

300. A large pen-and-ink drawing of the north exterior side of Stratford Church, executed about the year 1762.

301. The Mappe of Norfolke, Svffolke, Cambridgeshire, Bedford, Hartford, Buckingham, Oxford, Northampton, Warwick, Huntington and Leecestershires, and Rutland, part of Lincolne, Nottingham, Darbye, Glocester and Barckshires, and of the County of Essex. W. Hollar, 1644.

302. The Font at which Shakespeare was baptized. A coloured lithograph by J. Salmon from a drawing by Mrs. Dighton. Published at Stratford-on-Avon, 1835.

303. A large sketch taken by Blight in 1864, of the Wier Brake.—The kitchen and chimney-corner of Shakespeare's Birth-Place, from a sketch taken by Fairholt in August, 1839.

304. A view of the town and castle of Windsor from a painting at Greenwich Hospital executed about the year 1690.

305. Charlecote Church, from a sketch by Saunders, taken differently from No. 621.

306. A view of Exhall; St. Christopher, the hood-mould termination of the doorway leading from the chancel to the charnel-house, Stratford Church; a street in Wixford; a portion of the so-called Arden House at Wilmecote. All sketched by Blight in 1863.

307. The Road from Glocester to Coventrey, by Iohn Ogilby, esq., His Majesties Cosmographer, containing 58 miles 2 furlongs, viz., from Glocester to Cheltenham, to Winchcomb, through Broadway to Campden, to Stratford, to Warwick, to Coventrey, 1675.

308. A Mappe of Kent, Sovthsex, Surrey, Middlesex, Barke, and Southamptonshire, &c. Hollar's map of 1644, with roads added by a later hand. "Printed, coloured, and sold by Iohn Garrett, at the South Entrance of the Royall Exchange in London." See No. 299.

309. Warwici Comitatvs Descriptio, quam primus ædidit Christophorus Saxton anno 1576,

nunc de integro correcta, aucta et restituta ; cui adduntur (præter 60 locos qui priore desiderabantur) singula hundreda, viæ notiores, in vsum itinerantium accomodatæ, et alia non infimæ notæ nonnulla, anno 1603.—Near the corner is—Printed and sovld by P. Stent.—This is the earliest map of Warwickshire in which the roads are marked, Stent having, I believe, put or stamped his name as publisher to a plate of older date than the period at which he flourished.

310. Pen-and-ink views of Islip Church, co. Oxon, from photographs that were taken before the extensive alterations that were made about the year 1860. Islip was in one of the routes from Stratford to Oxford.

311. A pen-and-ink view of Middle-row, Stratford-on-Avon, from a photograph taken just previously to its removal in 1857.

312. The Counti of Warwick, the Shire Towne and Citie of Coventre described. Performed by Iohn Speede, and are to by solde in Popes-heade ally against the Exchange by Iohn Sudbury and George Humble, 1610.—No roads marked. There is a plan of Warwick in the left-hand corner and one of Coventry in the right.

313. Londinum Feracissimi Angliæ Regni Metropolis. An uncoloured copy of Braun's plan of London, 1574.

314. The title-page of Colloquia Physica Nova et Admiranda, 1614, with the autograph of Ben Jonson.

315. La Ville de Londres, an edition of Braun's map published at Paris in 1579. It was taken

from an engraving that was in the first and rare state of the plate, before the Royal Exchange was introduced.

316. A New Description of Kent divided into the fyue Lathes therof, and subdivided into Baylywickes and Hundredes, with the parishe Churches conteyned within euery of the same Hundredes. All which, for better vnderstandinge, are distinguished with varyetye of couloures: comprehendinge as well the cities, the vsuall market townes and the portes with their members lying in Kent; as also such of the howses of the nobylitie and gentrye as the plott coulde conueniently receaue. Wherin moreover the nature of the soyle, whether playne, hyllye or wooddye, is more diligentlye observed, and the tractes of ryuers, rylles and creekes, with the trendinge of the sea-shore, be more naturally described then heretofore it hath ben done. By the travayle of Phil: Symonson of Rochester, gent. Printed and sovld by P. Stent at the White Horse in Giltspure street, 1659.—At the top is a view of Dover by Hollar, and one of Rye by Sir Anthony Van Dyck, the latter showing the sea up to the town.

317. Anne Hathaway's Cottage, Shottery, drawn and etched by W. Rider. Published in November, 1827. A proof.

318. A front view of Charlecote House, in lithotint by F. W. Hulme from a sketch by J. G. Jackson. Published by Chapman and Hall in September, 1845.—The back of Charlecote House, from a drawing by Saunders.

319. Sketches taken by Blight, 1863 to 1865, of the well at Anne Hathaway's Cottage; the barn at the pseudo-Asbies farm-house at Wilmecote; a room on the basement at Anne Hathaway's Cottage, the one which is the furthest from the road, with the original stone-bench for the milk-pans; exterior, north side chancel, Stratford Church; interior of the door-way leading from the tower to the roof of the nave of the Guild Chapel; the basement wall of Nash's House.

320. Inside of charnel-house, Stratford Church, looking south, from a sketch by R. B. Wheler; Luddington Chapel, from a sketch by Dugdale; a large pike (or luce) from an old painting at Charlecote.

321. Interior of Anne Hathaway's Cottage, drawn and etched by W. Rider. Published in November, 1827. A proof.

322. The room in which Shakespeare was born, an uncoloured lithograph from a drawing by Mrs. P. Dighton. Published at Stratford-on-Avon in the year 1835.

323. Plan du Chateau et Parc de Windsor, dans la Conté de Berk, a 20 Milles de Londres, renferment une des maisons et jardins du Duc de Marlborough; tres exatement levé et gravé par J. Rocque, 1738.

324. A Plan of the Town and Castle of Windsor and Little Park, and the Town and College of Eton, survey'd and drawn by W. Collier. Publish'd according to Act of Parliament by W. Collier at Eton, 1742, by whom lands are survey'd and maps drawn of the same in the best and cheapest manner.

Sold by J. Pine, engraver in Old Bond Street, and T. Bakewell, printseller in Fleet Street. Engrav'd by J. Pine.—The very rare original engraving, being the earliest plan of Windsor Park in which Herne's Oak is noticed.

325. Three engraved ground-plans of New Place and the adjoining houses, six impressions only of which were taken previously to the destruction of the blocks.

326. A Mapp of Warwickshire, describing the Boundaries and Divisions, the Rivers, Brooks and Rills, the Roman Roads and Stations, the Parish Churches and Chapels, from an actual survey made in the year 1725 by Henry Beighton.

327. The Market-cross and part of High Street, Stratford, from a drawing by C. F. Green, 1821.

328. A large view of Charlecote House, copied in pen-and-ink from a photograph taken in 1864.

329. A View of the Antient Royal Palace, called Placentia, in East Greenwich. Publish'd according to Act of Parliament, April 23, 1767, sumpt. Societ. Antiquar.

330. A Prospect of the House att Windsor belonging to his Grace, Charles Beauclerck, Duke of St. Albans. L. Knyff de. I. Kip scu. This engraving includes curious and interesting views of the towns of Windsor and Eton.

331. Windsor Castle. Le Chasteau de Windsor. L. Knyff del. I. Kip sculp.—This view shows a good many of the old houses at Windsor about the year 1720.

332. A Plan of the Town and Castle of Windsor and Little Park, survey'd and drawn by W. Collier, 1742; the portion showing Herne's Oak from a varied impression of No. 324.

333. The East Prospect of Charlecote in Warwickshire, the Seat of the Reverend Wm. Lucy, esq., 1722. H. Beighton delin. 1722. E. Kirkall sculp.

334. The monumental effigy and oval portrait of Shakespeare on a pedestal, the latter engraved by Vander Gucht. From Rowe's Life of Shakespeare, 1709.

335. The interior of Charlecote Hall, a sketch by Mrs. Dighton, 1835; the original from which the lithograph was taken.

336. Prospect of Windsor Castle and Towne from South S. West. Prospect of the same Castle from West South West. Prospect of it from West and by South. W. Hollar delin. et sculp.

337. The Shakespeare Cliff, Dover. A large etching by one M. S., 1820.

338. Ciuitatis Westmonasteriensis pars. W. Hollar fecit, 1647.

339. Vindesorivm celeberrimum Angliæ castrum locus amoenissimus; ædificia magnifica; artificiosa Regum sepulchra, et illustris Garetteriorum equitum Societas memorabile reddunt. Depingebat Georgius Hoefnagle. Cum priuilegio. 1574.

340. The Old Stabling of the Three Pigeons, Brentford, "the inn frequented by Shakespeare and Ben Jonson." Drawn and etched by W. N Wilkins, June, 1848.

341. The back of the grammar-school, Stratford-on-Avon, a large water-colour sketch taken by Blight in 1864.

342. A large and curious sepia drawing of Windsor Castle and part of the town, executed about the year 1640.

343. Windsor Castle. W. Hollar delineavit et sculpsit.—This is a curious view, showing part of the ancient town in interesting detail.

344. Shakespeare's Tomb, a coloured lithograph from a sketch by Mrs. P. Dighton. Published at Stratford-on-Avon, 1835.

345. The College in Stratford-upon-Avon, in the county of Warwick, the seat of the Combe's, the Clopton's and the Keyte's, with their arms and quarterings.—A large view copied, about the year 1810, from some older drawing.

346. Sala Regalis cum Curia Westmonasterii, vulgo Westminster Hall. W. Hollar fecit, 1647.

347. Prospect of Windsor Castle from the North. Christopher Wren delineavit. W. Hollar fecit, 1667.—An interesting engraving, including detailed views of many of the old houses.

348. Two views of houses in the immediate neighbourhood of the Birth-Place, from photographs that were taken about the year 1854.—Interior of a room on the ground-floor of Anne Hathaway's Cottage, sketched by Blight in 1864.—The great hall at Charlecote in the state in which it was seen by Washington Irving, from a sketch by Fairholt.

349. Sketches taken by Blight in 1863 and 1864 of the Guild Chapel tower; the Council-Chamber and Grammar School; a baby-chair at Mrs. James's said to have been formerly at the Birth-Place; a cross at the west-end of Wixford-Church; a pinnacle of the Guild Chapel then (1864) lying on the roof of the porch; an old chimney at Wixford.

350. A Map of Barlichway Hundred, that in which Stratford-on-Avon is situated, reduced from an actual survey made, in the year 1725, by Henry Beighton.

351. Warwici Comitatus, a Cornauiis olim inhabitatus. Christophorus Saxton descripsitt, William Kip sculpsitt.—No roads shown.

352. Norden's original Plan of Middlesex, on a much larger scale and with numerous variations from the published engraving of 1593 (see No. 378).—This interesting survey was executed for Queen Elizabeth, Norden referring to "your Magesties howses" in the list of objects he has attached to the plan, and the Queen's arms being depicted in the left-hand corner. Norden was the first English surveyor who had any kind of pretension to scientific accuracy. His original manuscript plans are of great rarity, the present one of Middlesex and that of Essex, the latter in the possession of the Marquis of Salisbury at Hatfield, being the only ones known in private libraries.

353. The epitaph on the poet's widow, Anne Shakespeare, 1623, a full-sized tracing made by William Butcher, jun., 1885.

354. Sketches taken by Blight in 1864 of an ancient window and gable at Islip, and of the manor-house at Wheatley, both in co. Oxon.

355. An Ichnography of the Borough of Stratford-upon-Avon and the Village of Old Stratford, in the County of Warwick. A large original plan made by Jordan about the year 1780.

356. Charlecote Great Hall, a lithotint by F. W. Hulme from a sketch by J. G. Jackson. Published by Chapman & Hall, London, September, 1845.

357. Middlesex olima Trinobantibvs habitata, Johannes Norden descripsit. From Camden, 1607.—No roads shown.

358. A view of Stratford Church and river. Drawn by P. Dewint. Engraved by W. Radclyffe, Birmingham, 1824.

359. A large plan of Oxford and a small view of the town, 1649. An engraving of foreign execution.

360. Bridge at Hampton Lucy. Drawn by P. Dewint. Engraved by W. Radclyffe, 1825.

361. A Map of Middlesex, described by Iohn Norden, augmented by I. Speed, sold by Henry Overton at the White Horse without Newgate, London.—The main roads shown.

362. The exterior of the Birth-Place and the interior of the Birth-Room, sketches made by Mrs. Dighton in 1834, the originals from which the published lithographs of the following year were taken.

363. The Ground Plott of Warwick. W. Hollar fecit, 1654. From Dugdale's Warwickshire, 1656.

364. Herne's Oak, Windsor Park. Published for S. Ireland in May, 1799.

365. The Mapp of Barlichway Hundred, that in which Stratford-on-Avon is situated. Ro. Vaughan sculp. From Dugdale, 1656.

366. A Ground-Plan of Stratford Church, including that of the Charnel-house, with a scale of feet. Copied by Richard Greene, in the year 1765, from a drawing by S. Winter. The earliest known to exist.

367. A New Map, containing the Towns, Gentlemen's Houses, Villages and other Remarks round London, as from London to Windsor, Ware, Chelmsford, the Hope, Tunbridge, Guildford, &c. Maed and sold by H. Moll in Vanly's Court in Blackfryers.—A very elaborate map showing the main roads.

368. A large sketch in water-colours of Shakespeare's crab-tree and surrounding scenery. Believed to be a copy of an earlier view.

369. Two views of the crab-tree copied by Blight from rude originals that were taken about the year 1810. In reference to the second of these views the late Mr. W. O. Hunt thus wrote in 1864,—" the above drawing of the tree is very like what I remember of it when I passed some fifty-five years ago to school."

370. Interior of the Church of the Holy Trinity, Stratford-on-Avon. Printed by M. & N. Han-

hart. C. Graf, lith., London. Published by Edward Adams. A large view.

371. A tower and the exterior of adjoining rooms at Charlecote House, sketched by Blight in 1863.—A bird's-eye view of the mansion from an old painting in the hall that was executed about the year 1685.

372. Large sketches by Blight, taken in 1864, of the bedroom adjoining Anne Hathaway's, and of the upper room of the cottage next the road.

373. The South Side of Windsor Castle. Prospect of the Castle from the S.E.—Two long views by Hollar, c. 1670.—The first of these views contains, I believe, the earliest representation of the Church at which Anne Page was married.

374. The Clyff of Dover from Sea. This and another engraved sketch of Hollar's, No. 595, are the earliest views of Shakespeare's Cliff known to exist.

375. The prospect of Warwick from Coventre Roade on the North-east part of the Towne.—The prospect of it from London road on the south side of the Towne.—From Dugdale, 1656.

376. A long narrow view of London from the Surrey side of the river below the bridge. Hollar, c. 1641.

377. The Mapp of Canterbury. From Somner's Antiquities of Canterbury, 1640.

378. Myddlesex. Iohannes Norden Angl. descripsit, 1593.—This plan shows all the main roads. It is the diminutive published engraving,

a larger and more elaborate original plan being in this collection, No. 352.

379. The Droeshout portrait engraved on wood by J. T. Blight. The first proof.

380. The Monumental Effigy of Shakespeare. F. W. Fairholt. del. et sc., 1852. On India-paper.

381. An engraved view of Rochester, c. 1760.

382. Shakespeare's Tomb. An uncoloured lithograph from a drawing by Mrs. P. Dighton. Published at Stratford-on-Avon, 1835.

383. Vera effigies Ben Iohnsonii. Engraved by R. Vaughan, 1640.

384. Shakspeare. Engraved by T. A. Dean, after a drawing by A. Wivell, from the bust by Gerard Johnson, London. Published, 1827, by A. Wivell, Castle Street East. On large paper.

385. The second Sir Thomas Lucy, from a picture in the hall at Charlecote. A pencil copy by Blight from a pen-and-ink sketch by F. W. Fairholt.

386. The Monumental Effigy. G. Vertue sculp. 1725.

387. The Monumental Effigy, drawn by Mr. John Boaden from the Stratford Bust. Engraved by E. Scriven, 1825.

388. Shakespeare's Monument. Drawn by R. B. Wheler. Engraved by F. Eginton, Birmingham, 1806.

389. Mr. William Shakspeare his true Effigies, engraved by Wm. Ward, A.R.A., from a painting

by Thos. Phillips, esq., R.A., after a cast by G. Bullock from the bust at Stratford-on-Avon, 1816.

390. Effigies in the Clopton Chapel, Stratford-on-Avon. Two beautifully executed pencil drawings by J. T. Blight, 1864.

391. The Droeshout portrait of Shakespeare, 1623, on wood by Blight from the proof copy of that engraving. One of six impressions that were taken before the block was destroyed.

392. A large unfinished pencil sketch of the exterior of Stratford Church by J. T. Blight, and another, a finished one, taken by the same artist in 1863 from the eastern side of the river.

393. A sketch of Chapel Lane showing the cottage on the site of Getley's (afterwards Shakespeare's) copyhold estate. A recent copy of an earlier view.

394. An engraved portrait of the Earl of Essex, who was beheaded in 1601, and who was one of the patrons of Shakespeare's company. From an original painting then preserved at Essex House. Published by Holland in 1620.

395. Campden House, near London. 1795.

396. An East View of the Collegiate Church of Stratford-upon-Avon. A South-East view of the Col. Church of Stratford.—These drawings were made in or before the year 1763, and show the designs for a new steeple by Timothy Lightholder. They were, no doubt, although not so stated, made by Richard Greene in 1762.

397. Backs of old timber buildings in High Street, Stratford-on-Avon, the fronts of which

have been modernized. A sketch taken by Blight, 29 July, 1863.

398. Articles called Shakespeare's Jug and Cane, pencil sketches of the originals in the possession of Mrs. Fletcher of Gloucester.

399. A water-colour sketch, by Blight, of an ancient carved oak court-cupboard, formerly in the house said to have belonged to the Ardens at Wilmecote.

400. The Royal Pallace and Town of Windsor. Published by Cox, 1720.

401. Shakespeare's Cliff, Dover, from a sketch taken in 1843. F. W. Fairholt, sc.

402. An engraved portrait of Frederick, Duke of Wirtemberg, the Duke de Jarmany of the Merry Wives of Windsor, published in Germany in 1602.

403. Exterior of Anne Hathaway's Cottage, an original sketch by Mrs. Dighton, 1835.

404. Two coloured views, taken by Blight in 1864, of the ancient cellar at the Crown Inn, Rochester. Interesting medieval work. This tavern has since been either pulled down or completely modernized.

405. View of the House at Wilmcotte where Robert Arden resided whose daughter Mary was married to John Shakespeare. An engraved copy of an original sketch by Jordan, one of six copies only that were taken before the wood-block was destroyed.

406. A view of Broom, co. Warwick, the "beggarly broom" of the well-known verses.

An original sketch by the Rev. Richard Jago, vicar of Snitterfield, c. 1778.

407. A water-colour drawing of Shakespeare's crab-tree, as it appeared about the year 1822. A recent copy.

408. Windsor Castle. A water-colour drawing made about the year 1780. Artist's name unknown.

409. Old cottage at Shottery. Blight, 1863.

410. The West View of Welcombe Hills, publishd 1st. September, 1777, by S. Hooper, No. 25, Ludgate Hill. Some of the poet's land was situated on these hills.

411. A copy, in water-colour, of an oil painting, executed about the year 1690, of Windsor Castle, showing the houses by the river, and the entrance of the lane through which Falstaff was carried in the buck-basket. The large original painting, formerly in my possession, I gave many years ago to the Birth-Place Museum.

412. The font at which Shakespeare was baptized. An uncoloured lithograph from a drawing by Mrs. P. Dighton. Published at Stratford-on-Avon in 1835.

413. Charlecote Hall, drawn and etched by W. Rider. Published November 1st, 1827, by the artist and by J. Merridew, Leamington and Warwick. A proof.

414. Stratford Church, &c. Sam. Ireland del., 1792. This engraving shows also the river and the old mill.

415. The mark-signature and seal of George Whatcley, 1579, one of six impressions only that

were taken before the wood-block was destroyed. He was the bailiff of Stratford-on-Avon in the year of the poet's birth.

416. Ancient bridge over Brent Brook, near Hanwell, sketched by Blight in July, 1864.

417. Windsor Castle and Little Park. The royal carriage and attendants in the foreground. W. Hollar fecit, 1644.

418. Richmond Palace. M. Van de Gucht sculp.

419. Herne's Oak. T. Thornton del. Medland sculpsit. Published in June, 1792, by E. Harding.

420. "A View of Herne's Oak in the Little Park at Windsor," with part of Queen Elizabeth's Walk This original sketch, made by Hayman Rooke, an accurate topographer, about the year 1770, is the most interesting early drawing of the oak known to exist.

421. The porch and tower of the Guild Chapel, with part of the Falcon Tavern. John Johnson, F.S.A., del. A. Newman lith. Day & Son, lithographers to the Queen.

422. The ancient carved porch and gateway at the Crown Inn, Rochester, sketched by Blight in 1863. Now pulled down.

423. The old bridge at Islip, co. Oxon, A pencil sketch by Blight, 1864.

424. Sketches taken by Blight in 1863 of the ancient register-book of Stratford-on-Avon, showing the old binding and the clasps; and of an ancient Bible preserved in the Church.

425. Herne's Oak, 1788. A. E. H. pinxit. G. E. H. fecit. An etching.

426. Borealis Prospectus Ecclesiæ Stratfordiæ Super Avon in Comitatu Warwicenci. J. Gwin sc. Viro Reverendo Josepho Greene, Regiæ Scholæ in Stratfordia Moderatori, humillime inscribitur. c. 1740.—This is the earliest engraved view of the Church known to exist.

427. Sketches taken by Blight in 1864 of objects in Stratford Church,—an effigy in the Clopton Chapel; the old font; a doorway south side of the chancel.

428. A sketch from the sedilia in the Stratford Museum, formerly in the Chapel of St. Thomas in Stratford Church.

429. An exceedingly curious termination of the hood-moulding of a window on the north side of the chancel of Stratford Church, sketched by Blight in the year 1866.

430. An outline sketch by Blight, 1863, of part of the tower staircase in Stratford Church.

431. The entrance to Stratford Churchyard, showing the wooden bars on the ground to keep pigs from entering. A copy of an original sketch in the Saunders collection.

432. Original sketches taken by Blight, in 1863, of objects in the interior and on the exterior of Stratford Church,—a boss in the centre of the roof of the porch; the second and third windows east of porch in the north aisle; mouldings in the tower and south aisle.

433. A stone over the south window of transept in Stratford Church, and remains of mosaic pavement on the altar steps, copied from drawings by R. B. Wheler.

434. Original sketches, taken by Blight in 1863 and 1866, of objects in the interior and on the exterior of Stratford Church,—carvings on the canopies of sedilia in the Chapel of St. Thomas; tower window and turret, with a separate sketch of the roof of the latter; turret of staircase; parapet and gargoyle west of porch; hoodmould terminations of doorway leading from the chancel to the charnel-house; south window in tower; belfry doorway and window; the vicar's stall; windows in the north aisle, north transept, and south aisle.

435. A view of the Church and village of Hillingdon, sketched by Blight in 1864. This village is on the old road between Stratford-on-Avon and London.

436. An outline sketch by Blight of the south door in the south aisle of Stratford Church.

437. A very perfect specimen of a small timbered building of the sixteenth century at Little Alne, co. Warwick, a place where some of the poet's connexions once resided. Sketched by Blight in August, 1863.

438. Cantvarbvry. Cantvaria, vrbs fertilis simæ Angliæ celebris, Archiepiscopati sede, commendata. A curious plan of Canterbury, with part of the road to London, published by Braun in 1574.

439. Sketches by Blight, taken in 1864, of objects in Stratford Church,—the tower window and set-off of stage; the base of the tower arches;

four of the quaint and interesting carvings on the miserere stalls.

440. Prospects of Dover and Banbury, 1724. Stukeley delin. Toms et E. Kirkall sculp.

441. The Bridge and part of Bridge Street, Stratford-on-Avon. Drawn by R. B. Wheler. Engraved by F. Eginton, Birmingham. Published in May, 1806.

442. The Stratford Jubilee. Ireland, 1795.

443. Herne's Oak, 1788. A lithographic copy, published in 1820 by T. N.

444. The North Prospect of Trinity Church, Stratford-upon-Avon. R. Hickes fecit, 1737. A recent copy of an old drawing.

445. The left-hand cover of the old Register Book of Stratford-on-Avon; a copy of a sketch by Fairholt.

446. Sedilia in Stratford Church, a pencil sketch by Blight taken in 1863.

447. The Church at Barton-on-the-Heath, a sketch taken by Blight on the 6th of October, 1864. This place was the residence of the Lamberts, who were relatives of the poet.

448. Original sketches, taken by Blight in 1864, illustrative of Shakespeare's journeys between Stratford and London, viz., Tetsworth, West Wickham, the Crown Inn passage at Oxford, Stokenchurch, and the Three Pigeons.

449. A sketch taken by Blight in 1865 of a mermaid, from a miserere stall now in the Stratford Museum. It is said to have come from the Guild

Chapel, but no good authority has been given for the statement.

450. The Church. Drawn by R. B. Wheler. Engraved by F. Eginton, Birmingham. Published in May, 1806.

451. Sketches by Blight of objects at the Crown Inn, Oxford; the manor-house, Wheatley; Islip and Adderbury.

452. A large recumbent effigy in the Clopton Chapel, Stratford-on-Avon, sketched by Blight in the year 1864.

453. The upper part of an old pulpit formerly in Stratford Church. From an old painting made before the alterations of 1836.

454. A large recumbent figure in the Clopton Chapel; Blight, 1864.—The old pulpit, from the painting in the Church.

455. Sketches taken by Blight in 1864 of the exterior of the Birth-Place, and a view of the interior from the portrait-room looking towards the attic stairs.

456. Recumbent effigies of a gentleman and his wife, sketched by Blight from the originals in the Clopton Chapel, Stratford-on-Avon.

457. A recent copy of a view of Shakespeare's Crab-tree taken by C. F. Green in 1823.

458. Church Street, Oxford. A sketch, 1864.

459. A sketch of the roof of the nave of Stratford Church looking towards the tower. From a painting executed before the alterations of 1836.

460. The ancient bridge at Wixford, a copy of a sketch taken about the year 1810.

461. Curious old timbered houses in Bridge Lane, Warwick, one bearing the date of 1568. A sketch by F. W. Fairholt taken in 1847.

462. Sketches, taken by Blight in 1864, of localities illustrative of the journeys of Shakespeare, viz., Postcombe, Wheatley, and Burmington.

463. The George Inn, Uxbridge, a copy made in 1864 from an older sketch.

464. Sketches taken by Blight in 1864 of Pershore Bridge; a street in Acton; Steeple Aston Church from Hopcrofts Holt; an ancient stone fire-place in the Crown Inn at Oxford; old house at Deddington; the back of the Rein-deer Inn at Banbury.

465. Windsor Castle and part of the town, published by Cox, 1720. This view shows the river, and differs altogether from No. 400.

466. The effigies of William Clopton, esquier, and Anne his wiffe, daughter of Sir George Griffith, knight, 1592 and 1596. Dugdale, 1656.

467. Sketches taken by Blight in 1863 at Temple Grafton, Marston, and Barton.

468. West side of tomb in the south aisle, Stratford Church, a sketch by Blight, 1863.— The charnel-house, from a drawing by Wheler.

469. Sketches, taken by Blight in 1863, of objects in Stratford Church,—figures from the old roofs of the transepts; the canopy of a sedile; string-course under the windows in the north

transept ; a bit from the east side of the south transept ; the belfry of the tower ; exterior of the upper part of the tower ; wooden string-courses in the nave ; corbels in the south side of chancel.

470. Sketches taken by Blight in 1865, one of Stratton Audley and two of Grendon Underwood.

471. "A view of the publick house at Wilmcotte, where Robert Arden esq. lived, whose daughter Mary was married to John Shakespere," copy of a sketch by Jordan.

472. Sketches by Blight of the curious ancient misereres in Stratford Church ; the back of the Falcon Inn at Bidford ; and of a very old house near the Three Pigeons at Brentford.

473. An old wooden bridge that was formerly between Windsor and Eton, a copy made in 1863 from an early painting in the possession of Mr. G. Tuck of Windsor.

474. Old timbered house near Datchet, 1863.

475. Original sketches, taken by Blight in 1863, 1864, and 1865, illustrative of Shakespeare's journeys, viz., Warwick, Wixford, Marston, Eton, Bidford, Pebworth, Beaconsfield, Temple Grafton, Waddesdon, Pershore, and Grendon Underwood.

476. Elizabethan Gateway, St. Alban's, 1867.

477. Three sketches by Blight of objects in Stratford Church, one being the Chancel doorway leading to the Charnel House, taken in 1863.

478. Elizabethan house at Rochester, 1863.

479. Old timbered house at Tetsworth, 1864.

480. Shakespeare's Crab-tree, a woodcut from Ireland's Picturesque Views on the Avon, 1795.

481. A curious example of mosaic pavement on the altar steps of Stratford Church, from a drawing by R. B. Wheler.

482. Sketches taken by Blight in 1863 of a cornice in the south aisle of Stratford Church; window in the cellar of the Crown Inn, Rochester; and the entrance to Stratford Church.

483. The ancient stocks at Windsor Castle, a sketch taken by Fairholt in 1847.

484. Four elaborate water-colour drawings by J. C. Buckler, 1823, two of the exterior and two of the interior of Stratford Church.

485. Three interesting etchings of Dover and its castle. W. Hollar, 1643.

486. The roof of the nave of Stratford Church, looking east, as it appeared before the alterations of 1836, from the oil painting preserved at New Place.

487. Sketches by Blight in 1865 and 1866 of a wood carving in the Stratford Museum, said to have been originally placed either in the Church or in the Guild Chapel, and of the canopy of a sedile in the Chapel of St. Thomas, Stratford Church.

488. A large general view of Stratford-on-Avon taken by Blight in August, 1863, from the Hill, and an unfinished sketch of the Wier Brake taken in 1864.

489. View of the Clopton Bridge, the river, and the lower part of Bridge Street, from a painting of the last century.

490. A view of the ancient mill-bridge, the ait, and the river up to the Wier Brake, taken by Blight from the uttermost room of the mill.

491. Birth-Place sketches taken by Blight in 1864,—part of the front exterior ; under the stairs of the record-room ; the upper room of the same ; the butcher's shop.

492. The back of Mr. Hunt's house in Church Street, as it is believed to have been when possessed by the Cloptons. A conjectural resuscitation, but founded on an examination of the remains of the ancient timber-work.

493. Sketches by Blight, 1863 and 1864, of the end of the Birth-Place ; the mill-bridge ; the panelling in the attic at the Birth-Place.

494. The shop at the Birth-Place, an interior looking to street, from a sketch by Fairholt.—The bacon cupboard at Anne Hathaway's Cottage, 1697, sketched by Blight in 1864.—The shop at the Birth-Place, an interior looking towards kitchen, from the sketch made by Fairholt for his Home of Shakespere.

495. Four views of the mill-bridge at Stratford, taken by Blight from different positions in 1864.

496. Sketches taken by Blight in 1863 and 1864 of the interior of Anne Hathaway's Cottage ; a grate in the possession of Mrs. James, brought from the Birth-Place ; Elizabethan houses at Henley-in-Arden.

497. An elaborate view of the front exterior of Charlecote House, taken about the year 1762, and believed to be the work of one Rogers, a Birmingham drawing-master.

498. Sketches taken by Blight in 1863 and 1864 of a room on the right-hand of the entrance to Anne Hathaway's Cottage; the room behind the shop at the Birth-Place; the entrance to the chimney in the room in that building now used for the Museum; the interior of the old panelled room at Abington Abbey, the residence of Shakespeare's grand-daughter.

499. Old Settle at Anne Hathaway's Cottage, from a sketch by F. W. Fairholt.—The Market-Cross, with the timbered corners of Wood Street and Henley Street, Stratford-on-Avon, from a drawing by C. F. Green, 1821.—The interior of the College Hall, Stratford-on-Avon, copied from a drawing made by Jordan about the year 1790.

500. The tomb of Sir Thomas Lucy in Charlecote Church, an elaborate sketch made by Blight in the year 1863.

501. The Shakespeare Inn, Shottery, in its old timbered state, a copy of a sketch made by Fairholt in 1847.

502. The Elizabethan carved oak bedstead at Anne Hathaway's Cottage, and the Birth-Place Museum, sketches taken by Blight in 1863.

503. Henley-in-Arden. Blight, 1864.

504. The Grammar-School, Stratford-on-Avon. Five sketches, consisting of two original ones by Blight, 1864, and three others copied by him from drawings by Fairholt.

505. Six large sketches taken by Blight in 1864, of portions of the Birth-Place,—the birth-room; the attic staircase; the room on the ground-floor

next the garden ; the exterior from the garden ; the apartment over the record-room, and decayed timber showing old mortices.

506. A general view of Stratford-on-Avon showing the Bancroft, a copy of a drawing made by R. B. Wheler about the year 1800.

507. Four large sketches, taken by Blight in 1864, of portions of the Birth-Place,—the exterior from the east of garden ; the attic ; the butcher's shop, and the museum.

508. Five large sketches taken by Blight in 1863 and 1864 of,—the mill-bridge ; the upper room of the Swan and Maidenhead, now the museum ; the interior of the school-room ; another view of the upper room of the museum ; a water-colour drawing of the attic at the Birth-Place.

509. Whitehall and Lambeth. Hollar, c. 1650.

510. The Birth-Room, from a sketch taken by Fairholt, 29 August, 1839.

511. The cottage at Anne Hathaway's at the end furthest from the road, a sketch by Blight, 1864, showing the dairy doorway and the lower part of an old cheese-press serving as a flag-stone.

512. Sketches by Blight, taken in 1864, of the bass-relief of David and Goliah formerly at the Birth-Place ; the Elizabethan house in the High Street, Stratford.

513. A south-west view of the collegiate Church, Stratford-on-Avon, R. Greene del., 1762. One of the earliest drawings of the Church known to exist.

514. Exterior of Stratford Church, a large pencil sketch taken about the year 1830.

515. A large coloured sketch by Blight, taken in 1864, of one of the attics in Anne Hathaway's Cottage.

516. A water-colour drawing of the Clopton Bridge, Stratford-on-Avon, by Rogers, a Birmingham schoolmaster, c. 1762.

517. Five large engraved views of the old St. Paul's Cathedral, two of the exterior and three of the interior. Wenceslaus Hollar delineavit et sculpsit, 1656, 1658.

518. Sketches by Blight of the lower stairs at the Birth-Place leading to the birth-room, with portions of the adjoining walls; the interior of the Hall of the Middle Temple, where Twelfth Night was performed in the year 1602; the old gateway, Charlecote.

519. Bearley Church, from a drawing c. 1810.

520. An elaborate coloured view of the screen and roof of the Hall in the Middle Temple, executed by Blight in 1867.—A cornice of figure heads in the Elizabethan house in the High Street, Stratford-on-Avon, sketched by the same artist in 1864.

521. A copy of an old sketch in water-colours formerly preserved in the Daniel library, and described as an "original drawing of the Stratford Jubilee, 1769," but it is evidently of a later date, executed probably about the year 1800.

522. Sketches taken by Blight in 1864 of a lock brought from the Birth-Place and then in the pos-

session of Mrs. James; of the portrait-room at the Birth-Place and the little room on the ground-floor near the garden.

523. A sketch of a box of crab-tree wood which appears to have belonged to one John Jordan of Stratford-on-Avon in 1646, but it has been suspected that the inscriptions to that effect were forged by his namesake of the last century. There was, however, a John Jordan living at Stratford about the time above-mentioned, as appears from a document in the Court of Record Papers, iv. 253.

524. A sketch by Blight, 1864, of a bridge on the road between Hillingdon and Uxbridge, the arches of which are of great antiquity. This bridge would have been passed over by Shakespeare in his journeys between London and Stratford.

525. Two views of the exterior of the back of the Birth-Place, copied from photographs that were taken previously to its restoration.

526. Sketches taken by Blight in 1864 of the birth-room and the record-room; portions of a bedstead said to have been brought from the Birth-Place; the little niche opposite the portrait-room; a carved desk at Mrs. James's, said to have been formerly in the Birth-Place; the large desk absurdly stated to be the one that was used by Shakespeare at school; two large views of the attic at the Birth-Place.

527. A long view of London, showing the Globe and other old theatres, with views of the exterior and interior of St. Paul's Cathedral. D.

King delin. et excudit, anno 1658. This engraving is evidently based on some unknown copies of earlier drawings.

528. A large water-colour drawing of old houses in the Mill Lane, Stratford-on-Avon, executed about the year 1820.

529. Braun's plan of London, 1574. Coloured. One of the very rare impressions from the plate in its first state, before the Royal Exchange was introduced.

530. Birth-Place illustrations,—its elevation as restored; plan before the restoration, showing the timbers of the original first floor; a full-sized plan of the ancient wrought-iron fastening to the birth-room window; a ground-plan taken shortly before the restoration; a copy of a view of the exterior, taken by John Sharp, c. 1790.

531. A Map or Ground Plot of the Citty of London and the Suburbes thereof, that is to say, all which is within the Iurisdiction of the Lord Mayor or properlie calldt London, by which is exactly demonstrated the present condition thereof since the last sad accident of fire, the blanke space signifeing the burnt part, and where the houses are exprest, those places yet standing. Sould by Iohn Overton at the White Horse in Little Brittaine, 1666.

532. A long view of London engraved abroad in the year 1649, with forty-three references to numbers. The Swan, the Bear Garden, and the Globe Theatre are in the foreground. This engraving is frequently assigned to Hollar, but the Guildhall copy is ascribed in manuscript to Matthew Merian.

533. A View of London from Howel's Londinopolis, 1657, with forty-six references to numbers. It is a copy of some earlier drawing, the Globe and other theatres being shown.—" London, the glory of Great Britaines ile,—Behold her landschip here, and tru pourfile."

534. Exterior of the Middle-Temple Hall, 1720.

535. The Prospect of Kenilworth Castle from the old parke; the prospect thereof upon the road from Coventrie; the prospect thereof upon Bull-hill neere the road from Colshill towards Warwick. Dugdale, 1656.

536. Bidford Bridge, from a sketch taken about the year 1810.

537. The wooden cornice of the lower room (now destroyed) of the Crown Inn, Rochester, a sketch by Blight, 1864. The woodwork is of a very heavy character.

538. Three sketches by Blight, one taken at Barton-on-the-Heath in 1864, and two at Wixford in 1863.

539. London and Westminster, two plans; Ioannes Norden Anglus descripsit, 1593. The first of these plans shows the Rose Theatre, the only regular one then on the south of the Thames, and that in which Shakespeare's earliest dramas were produced. It gives a more accurate idea than any other of the metropolis as it existed in the poet's time.

540. Later copies, "augmented" by Speed, 1610, of the two last views, that of London showing two theatres in Southwark.

541. The Visit of the Queen of Sheba to Solomon, and the victory of Constantine over Mexentius; Fisher's original coloured copies of paintings in the chancel of the Guild Chapel.

542. The Invention of the Holy Cross, two paintings on the north side of the Chancel of the Guild Chapel. Fisher del.

543. The Combat of Heraclius with the son of Cosdroy, King of Persia, and the decapitation of Cosdroy by Heraclius. Paintings discovered on the north side of the Chancel of the Guild Chapel. Fisher del.

544. The painting of St. George and the Dragon on the west wall of the nave of the Guild Chapel, north of the entrance. Fisher del.

545. The Judgment of the Whore of Babylon, a painting on the west wall of the nave of the Guild Chapel, north of the entrance and below St. George and the Dragon. Fisher del.

546. Figures on the porch; arms on the spandrils of the north door, and carved work on the spandrils of the south door, both of the latter within the Church. Original drawings by Fisher, 1804. These do not appear to have been engraved.

547. Exterior of Anne Hathaway's Cottage, a small flock of sheep and a dog in the foreground. C. Graf lith., London. Published by F. and E. Ward, 1851. Taken from a drawing made by an Edinburgh artist in 1850. This plate was republished by Adams as "printed by M. and N. Hanhart."

548. A view of the Birth-Place, c. 1835. Drawn, printed and published by G. Rowe, Cheltenham.

549. Shakespeare's Birth-Room, from a sketch by E. T. Parris, 1864.

550. Interior Views of Grammar School-rooms in which Shakespeare was educated; also the Guild Room and the Council Chamber; from original sketches by H. B. Clements.

551. Exterior of the Birth-Place. C. Graf. lith. Published by F. and E. Ward. When the Wards issued this engraving in 1851, it was expressly stated to have been taken from an original drawing.

552. A large view of the exterior of the Birth-Place, "engraved by Alfred Baker, aged 13 years, from a sketch taken in 1804." London, published for Alfred Baker by Colnaghi and Co.

553. The South Prospect of the Church of St. Saviour in Southwark. R. West delin., 1737. W. H. Toms sculp. Published in March, 1739.

554. Stratford Church, the River and the Mill Bridge, copies of paintings executed about the year 1710.

555. A View of London, taken in or before the year 1613, showing the old Globe Theatre. Published by Holland in 1620.

556. The House in which Shakespeare was born. An uncoloured lithograph from a drawing by Mrs. P. Dighton, published at Stratford-on-Avon in 1835.

557. A plan of commercial designs on the eastern side of the river at Stratford-on-Avon, as projected by Andrew Yarranton, 1677.

558. Exterior of Anne Hathaway's Cottage, an uncoloured lithograph from a drawing by Mrs. P. Dighton, 1835.

559. The exterior of the Birth-Place. Two joints of meat hanging under the shop pentice, and one on the outer board; post on extreme right-hand corner; a little more than half of the western cottage shown. A lithograph c. 1830.

560. A coloured facsimile of Norden's plan of Windsor and the Little Park, 1607.

561. The Birth-Place, drawn from nature, and on stone, by J. Brandard. Day and Haghe, lithographers to the Queen. Published by C. Elston, Leamington.

562. Shakespeare's Desk at Stratford-on-Avon, "still to be seen in the Grammar School where he received his education." An uncoloured lithograph from a drawing by Mrs. P. Dighton, published in 1835.

563. A plan of Norwich, xvii. Cent.

564. The inn yard, Rochester, and Shakespeare's Cliff, sketches taken by Fairholt about the year 1847.

565. Two sketches, taken by Blight in 1863 and 1864, one of the exterior of Stratford Church from Mr. W. O. Hunt's river-garden; the other of ancient houses and the Church at Beaconsfield.

566. The back of Charlecote Hall. Drawn from nature and on stone by J. Brandard. Leamington, published by C. Elston.

567. Middle Row and Bridge Street, c. 1835; a copy by Blight of a drawing by the late Mrs.

E. F. Flower, an interesting sketch exhibiting details nowhere else to be found.

568. The kitchen in Anne Hathaway's Cottage, a copy of a sketch taken by Fairholt about the year 1847.

569. Sketches by Blight of an ancient passage in Windsor Street, Stratford-on-Avon, 1864, and of the pulpit in Alderminster Church, said to have been brought from Stratford, and to have been the one presented to the latter town by the poet's son-in-law, John Hall.

570. Exterior of the Birth-Place before the restoration. W. L. Walton, 1861. M. and N. Hanhart, lith.

571. The room in which Shakespeare was born. J. Brandard lith. Sold only at the Shakespeare House. A reduced copy of No. 717.

572. The Sword of State anciently borne before the Mayor of Stratford-on-Avon. Blight, 1864.

573. Exterior of the Birth-Place. A coloured lithograph showing the whole of the Swan and Maidenhead, and the cottages on the left. A gentleman and lady in the foreground opposite the Birth-Place, the former pointing it out with his stick to the latter.

574. Exterior of the Birth-Place. A large unfinished etching, c. 1810, showing the Swan and Maidenhead before that inn was refronted. A man leading a horse, a dog preceding him, in the foreground. Very rare, if not unique.

575. A view of the Birth-Place and Henley Street, from a photograph taken shortly before

the restoration, and soon after the buildings adjoining the Birth-Place had been removed.

576. The Church at Billesley, a copy of an original sketch taken about the year 1810.

577. The back of the Birth-Place, a small portion of the west of that building with the adjoining cottages in Henley Street, and two views of the exterior, all being copies of original photographs taken shortly before the restoration.

578. The Mill-Bridge, Stratford-on-Avon, and the Cross-on-the-Hill, a sketch by Blight taken in August, 1864.

579. A Prospect of Warwick, July 7th, 1725. Stukeley del.

580. A plan of Stratford-on-Avon by Samuel Winter, 1759. The date, which is not annexed, is ascertained by the following note in the Joseph Greene manuscripts, the houses-number corresponding,—" in the year 1759 a careful survey of the town was taken, and an exact plan of the same delineated; when the number of houses therein was found to be 552." This is the earliest complete plan of the town known to exist, and as the site of New Place is marked as a house, it must have been made early in the above-mentioned year, that in which the mansion was pulled down by Gastrell. A later plan by the same surveyor, with a larger display of houses, preserved in the Stratford Museum, was probably taken about the year 1768.

581. Sketches taken by Blight, 1863 to 1865, of the back of the Birth-Place; objects in the north transept of Stratford Church and the west

window of the same edifice; the old font, Charlecote; a recess in the south wall of the nave near the chancel arch of the Guild Chapel; base mouldings, tower arch of the same Chapel; backs of old houses in the High Street, Stratford-on-Avon; the White Swan tavern in the Rother Market; a loop in the wall adjoining the moat of Shottery manor-house; a handle, a scutcheon of wood and a catch for a latch, from the refuse of the Birth-Place.

582. Interior of Gray's Inn Hall, 1804. The Comedy of Errors was performed in this Hall in the year 1594.

583. An unlikeness of Shakespeare in an engraved miniature; Gaywood fecit, 1655. As Wivell correctly observes, "the scarcity alone makes it valuable."

584. Exterior of the Birth-Place, c. 1849. A copy.

585. A sketch by Blight, 1863, of a portion of the tower arch, Guild Chapel.

586. Mortlake Church, J. Peak sc. Shakespeare's company were at this village in 1603.

587. Ancient door of the Church of Weston-on-Avon, a sketch by Fairholt, 1846.

588. A south-east view of Bishopton Chapel in the parish of Old Stratford, an original drawing in sepia by Richard Greene, c. 1762.

589. Charlecote Church, a sketch by J. J. Jackson, 1845.

590. Baynard's Castle, from a view of Old London painted by Claude de Jongh in 1650.

591. Exterior of the charnel-house, Stratford-on-Avon, from a drawing made by R. B. Wheler, c. 1810.—The Golden Lion and White Lion Inns, Stratford-on-Avon, from sketches taken about the year 1820.

592. The Church of Atherston-upon-Stour, near Stratford-on-Avon, an original drawing by Richard Greene, c. 1762.

593. A view of London from Tootehill Fields. Hollar, 1641.

594. Sketches by Blight, 1864, of two pieces of old wood found amongst the refuse of the Birth-Place, and a hood-mould termination, square light, north side of tower, Guild Chapel.

595. The Clyff of Dover, W. Hollar fecit. This and No. 374 are the earliest known views of Shakespeare's Cliff.

596. Sketches by Blight, 1864, of pieces of old timber found among the refuse of the Birth-Place; the exterior of Stratford Church; and the front of a grate that was formerly in the attic of the Birth-Place.

597. The pinnacles of the Guild Chapel, a recent copy of a sketch taken by Wheler.

598. Sketches by Blight, 1864, of a portion of a grate that was formerly in the attic at the Birth-Place, and the spandril of an arch over the doorway of the Guild Chapel.

599. The font and piscina at Bishopton Chapel, from a drawing made by R. B. Wheler.—Weston-on-Avon Church, a sketch by Fairholt, 1846.

600. Exterior of the Birth-Place, drawn and engraved by J. Storer, 1818. Perhaps the earliest engraving in which the Swan and Maidenhead is shown with the modern brick front.

601. The House at Stratford in which Shakespeare lived. A. Smith, sculp. London, printed for J. Bell, 1786. A copy of Greene's view.

602. A south-west view of Alveston Church, near Stratford-on-Avon, an original drawing by Richard Greene, c. 1762.

603. A minute sketch of an old theatre in the engraved title-page of the Tragedy of Messalina by N. Richards, 1640.

604. A piece of carved wood in the Birth-Place Museum, said to have been formerly part of a doorway at the Guild Chapel. A sketch by Blight, 1865.

605. An east prospect of the College in Stratford, 1765. The earliest view of this building known to exist.

606. Sketches by Blight, 1863 and 1867, of an ancient carved figure on the top of a pillar at the Crown Inn, Rochester, and of the silver paten at Bishopton Chapel, the circular enclosure of the date, 1571, being the exact size of the original.

607. The Mill-Bridge, Stratford-on-Avon, when in process of demolition, from a photograph taken in the year 1867.

608. Shakespeare's Birth-Place as it appeared previous to 1769, published by Henry Merridew, Coventry.

609. Stratford Church, exterior. C. F. Green lithog., c. 1820.

610. Charlecote House, the river front. Drawn by J. Roe. Engraved by J. and H. S. Storer. Published by Sherwood & Co., 1823. The late R. B. Wheler, in a letter dated in the same year, bears testimony to the accuracy of this view, observing, at the same time, that Ireland's sketch "from nearly the same point is rather incorrect."

611. A house in High Street, Stratford-on-Avon, 1829, a pen-and-ink drawing by Captain Saunders.—Henley Street, a copy of a sketch by the same. The latter shows the corner of the old timbered workhouse.

612. A sketch, taken by Blight in 1867, of the silver chalice in Bishopton Church. It measures $5\frac{1}{8}$ inches in height.—The ancient silver paten in the Church of Clifford-Chambers, near Stratford-on-Avon.

613. Shakespeare's House as it appeared in 1787.—Shakespeare's House as it now appears, 1837. Woodcuts from the Casket of April the 23rd, 1837.

614. The House in which Shakespeare was born. J. Archer del., W. Finden sc.

615. Exterior of the Birth-Place. An engraving of the house and inn as they appeared about the year 1810. Poultry and a fat child in the foreground. The letter S seen in a compartment over the window of the butcher's shop. A different view from that in the Mirror, 1823, in which the S is also found in the same place, but is less conspicuously exhibited.

616. An ancient door in the house in the Old Town which is believed to have been the residence of John Hall, the poet's son-in-law. Sketched by Blight, 1864.

617. North-west view of Stratford College, an engraving, 1808.

618. A diminutive map of Warwickshire, 1643.

619. An oval view of Stratford-on-Avon, c. 1720, a pencil drawing taken from an old painting.

620. Moll Cutpurse. "Mistress Mall's picture," Twelfth Night, i. 3. The extremely rare original engraving, not the reprint, from the Life and Death of Mrs. Mary Frith, commonly called Mall Cutpurse, 1662. This notorious character was born in 1584 and died in 1659.

621. Charlecote Church, a copy from Saunders.

622. Old timbered house in the Rother Market. Blight, 1864.

623. A piece of wood-carving in the Birth-Place Museum, said to have been formerly in the College. Sketched by Blight in 1865, it having been then in the possession of Miss Wheler.

624. Shakespeare's Birth-Place, exterior. T. G. Flowers, Edinburgh.

625. Houses in Henley Street, Stratford-on-Avon, including the Birth-Place. W. Alexander del. 1820.

626. A sketch by Blight, 1865, of a scroll of stone-work in the Clopton Chapel, Stratford Church.

627. A small view of the Birth-Place, copied from Saunders' illustrations to Washington Irving's paper on Stratford-on-Avon.

628. Figures from the Guild Chapel, sketches copied by Blight from drawings by R. B. Wheler.

629. A curious little view of an old English theatre in the engraved title-page of the tragedy of Roxana, 1632.

630. Figures formerly at Stratford College, copies by Blight from drawings by R. B. Wheler.

631. The Birth-room. T. G. Flowers, Edinburgh.

632. The Market-cross, from a drawing by Saunders.

633. Daisy Hill, a farm-house in which Shakespeare is mendaciously said to have been imprisoned. Ireland, 1795.

634. Two engraved views of the exterior of the Birth-Place, the first from the Mirror of January, 1823, the other from the Monthly Magazine of February, 1818.

635. Charlecote Vicarage, an old timbered house, drawn by P. Dewint, engraved by W. Radclyffe. Birmingham, 1823.

636. The back of Anne Hathaway's Cottage, from a sketch taken by Fairholt in 1847.

637. The Birth-Place, 1847. W. J. Linton sc.

638. Alveston Church and old timbered house, 1837, sketched from nature and on stone by Mrs. Bracebridge. Day and Haghe, lithographers to

the King. These are in the immediate neighbourhood of Stratford-on-Avon.

639. Anne Hathaway's Cottage, from a sketch taken by Fairholt in 1847.—Another view, C. F. Green del., c. 1820.

640. Charlecote Park, drawn and engraved by T. Radclyffe, 1829.—The Keeper's Lodge, Fulbroke Park, drawn and etched by W. Rider, 1827; a proof.

641. Interior of the Middle Temple Hall, published by Vernor and Hood, 1804.

642. Copies by Blight of sketches of the interior of Aston Cantlowe Church, the so-called Arden house at Wilmecote and Bishopton Chapel.

643. A series of sketches by Blight of objects at Wilmecote (including two interiors of the Arden house), Hampton Lucy, the Dingles, Snitterfield, Bearley and Aston Cantlowe.

644. Interior of the College Hall, from a drawing by R. B. Wheler; interior of Aston Cantlowe Church, a sketch by Blight, 1863.

645. Window, finial, and crocket in the Guild Chapel, original sketches by Blight.

646. The Birth-Place as it appeared at one of the jubilees, and a small portion of an Elizabethan house in Henley Street, from drawings by Captain Saunders.

647. Original sketches by Blight of panelling with moulded wood found amongst the refuse from the attic at the Birth-Place; interior perforated work of an ancient dove-cote at Wilmecote; end of an

old timbered building at the same place; grotesque carved heads in the Guild Chapel; old timbered house near the Grammar School, 1862; ancient deed-boxes in the record-room; arms on the Stratford-on-Avon maces; distemper paintings in the gable over the Council Chamber, 1863.

648. Old house at the bottom of Church Street, from a drawing by Captain Saunders.

649. Original sketches by Blight of pieces of old timber taken from the Birth-Place; the stocks at Stratford-on-Avon, 1864; interior of the old Council-Chamber, 1863.

650. Corner of old house near the Town Hall, from a sketch by Captain Saunders.

651. Original sketches by Blight of an old timbered house at Shottery; the old thatched tavern at the corner of Greenhill Street and the Rother Market, Stratford-on-Avon; passage leading out of Henley Street; ancient house at Wilmecote; old house in Meer Street, Stratford-on-Avon; a cottage at Wilmecote; old houses in Ely Street and Church Street, Stratford-on-Avon; rustic cottage at Wilmecote; the back of the Grammar-School, and the upper room of the schoolmaster's house, Stratford-on-Avon; a hood-mould termination and other objects at the Guild Chapel; old house in Henley Street, near the Market Cross; a panel and door found amongst the refuse taken from the Birth-Place.

652. Exterior of the Birth-Place, 1848, a copy by Blight of a sketch by F. Goodall, R.A.

653. A view of Aston Cantlowe, taken by Blight in 1863.

654. An original drawing of the exterior of the Birth-Place, executed by Richard Greene about the year 1762. It is the earliest representation of the house known to exist.

655. Charlecote and Daisy Hill, copies by Blight of sketches by Captain Saunders.

656. Original sketches, taken by Blight in 1864, of two figures in the 1596 house in High Street, Stratford-on-Avon; the doorway south side of nave, Guild Chapel; the monumental tablet erected to the memory of George and Esther Hart, 1696.

657. Two sketches, taken by Blight in July, 1863, of old houses in Shottery.—Elizabethan houses in Wood Street, from a sketch taken by the late Mrs. E. F. Flower, c. 1838.—The old font, Bishopton, a sketch by Blight, 1867.

658. Stratford Church, river and mill, from a painting executed about the year 1720. This was the date assigned to it from the costume by the late Mr. Planché.

659. The monumental effigy, front and side views. E. Blore del. Thompson sc.

660. Henley Street and the old timbered work-house, from a sketch taken by the late Mrs. E. F. Flower, c. 1835.

661. Snitterfield Church, from a drawing by Fairholt.—An engraved view of the same Church, S.E., Allan E. Everitt del., J. Brandard lith., published by H. T. Cooke, Warwick.

662. John Combe, taken from his monument in the Church of Stratford-upon-Avon. Drawn and etched by S. Harding, 1793.

663. An engraved view of Clopton House, published in 1829.

664. The western end of the Guild Chapel, a sketch taken by Blight in 1863.

665. The Elizabethan house in the High Street, Stratford-on-Avon. F. W. Fairholt del. C. D. Laing sc.

666. Portrait of Florio, 1611. Gul. Hole sculp.

667. Sketches, taken by Fairholt in 1847, of a carved wooden impost at the New Inn, Gloucester, and of the ancient cross and old houses at Henley-in-Arden.—The interior of the sexton's cottage, a curious old room, Stratford-on-Avon, from a sketch by Saunders.—The staircase at the Birth-Place, a sketch by Blight, 1864.

668. Exterior of the Birth-Place. Part of the Swan and Maidenhead, all the cottages on the left and a small portion of the White Lion Inn shown. An original water-colour drawing by Shepherd.

669. S. Marie Over's in Southwarke. W. Hollar fecit, 1647.

670. The Middle Temple Hall, 1803.

671. Sketches taken by Blight in 1863 of a cottage at Shottery; old barn in Greenhill Street; a view of Marsh Gibbon; the moated grange at Milcote; Barcheston (or Barson) Church, near Shipston-on-Stour; the Church at Clifford-Chambers.

672. Bearley Church, from a sketch by Saunders. —Barton-on-the-Heath, a sketch by Fairholt.

673. Sketches taken by Blight in 1863 of Welford and its maypole; old desk from Stratford College; the Windmill Inn, Church Street, Stratford-on-Avon; seal of Richard Quiney, 1592, the exact size of the original; old house and staircase, Grendon Underwood.

674. A pencil sketch of the Combe monument in Stratford Church, c. 1820. The artist's name unknown.

675. Exterior of the Birth-Place and part of Henley Street. London, J. Harwood, 1847.

676. The back of the Shakespeare Tavern, Shottery, from a sketch taken by F. Goodall, R.A., in July, 1848.

677. Sketches taken by Blight in 1863, of the Prince of Wales's Inn, Rother Street, Stratford-on-Avon; the upper room of the manor-house, Shottery; ancient gateway on the north of Chapel Street, Stratford-on-Avon; Charlecote Park; Anne Hathaway's bed-chamber and exterior of cottage.

678. The back of the Birth-Place, from a sketch taken by Fairholt in 1847.

679. The Birth-Place and the Swan. H. Fitzook del.

680. A room in Anne Hathaway's Cottage, 1847. W. J. Linton sc.

681. The Charnel House, Stratford-on-Avon, exterior and interior, from copies by Saunders of early drawings.

682. Sketches taken by Blight in 1863 of the back of Shottery manor-house; the interior of a

room in the supposed John Hall's residence in the Old Town, Stratford-on-Avon, and a view of Shottery from the Evesham Road.

683. The old timbered school-house at Snitterfield, 1825.—The foot-bridge near Anne Hathaway's Cottage, from a sketch taken by Fairholt in 1842.—The shop at the Birth-Place, from a drawing by Saunders.

684. Sketches, taken by Blight in 1863 and 1864, of an old timbered house adjoining the workhouse in Henley Street, and the mud-wall of an old barn near the Old Thatched Tavern, Stratford-on-Avon.

685. The birth-room, from a sketch by Saunders. —A sketch by Blight of a tower at Charlecote from the old painting in the hall, and of mouldings at the gateway.—Old buildings at Stratford-on-Avon that were removed when the new market-place was built, and interior of Bishopton Church, from sketches by Saunders.—Ancient house in the Rother Market, a sketch by Blight, 1864.

686. Shakespeare's grave-stone and inscription, with the dimensions of the stone, a lithograph from a drawing by Saunders, published by Ward of Stratford-on-Avon, 1827.

687. The Indian in his boat, the one brought over to England about the year 1580, and afterwards embalmed. Supposed to be alluded to in the Tempest. A contemporary German engraving of great rarity.

688. Hood-moulds in the large west window of the tower of the Guild Chapel, sketched by Blight in 1864.—Ancient timbered house at Birmingham,

1576, a sketch taken by Fairholt previously to its destruction in 1849.—A piece of old timber from the Birth-Place and the W.S. ring, two sketches by Blight.—The tomb and effigies of Sir Thomas and Lady Lucy in Charlecote Church, copied by my daughter Charlotte from a sketch by Saunders.

689. Sketches, taken by Blight, 1862 to 1867, of the Stratford-on-Avon maces; old house in Bridge Street, Stratford-on-Avon; interior of room in the tower of Charlecote gatehouse; ancient knocker on the door of house near the grammar-school, Stratford-on-Avon; a dormer window in Turnmill (Turnbull) Street, London, the only fragment of old work remaining there in 1865; the stone-carved sign of the Cock-and-Pye tavern at Bewdley, and another one, also in stone, of St. George and the Dragon at Snow Hill, London, these two signs being interesting relics of the taverns of the Shakespearean period.

690. Bishopton Chapel and the old school-house, Snitterfield, copies of sketches taken by Captain Saunders.

691. Sketches by Blight, 1863 to 1865, of an old house and the Church at Aston Cantlowe; the porch of Welford Church; steps, doorway, and end of Anne Hathaway's Cottage; a piece of decayed timber found amongst the refuse of the Birth-Place; south door of Chapel in the manor-house, Shottery; back of Anne Hathaway's Cottage; old houses at Bishopton and Aston Cantlowe.

692. Welford Church Porch, a sketch by Fairholt.

693. Sketches by Blight, taken in 1863 and and 1864, of Long Lane, near Stratford-on-Avon; old houses at Clifford-Chambers; Pathlow Hill farm-house; old cottages by the Water Side, Stratford-on-Avon.

694. Shakespeare's Desk. Rev. R. Nixon, F.S.A., del. 1824. Fahee lithog. Printed by C. Hullmandel. Published by J. Ward.

695. The Birth-Place, c. 1805, a copy; old houses in Church Street, Stratford-on-Avon, a sketch taken by Blight in 1863.

696. Two views of Charlecote House, taken on 22 August, 1823. Name of artist unknown.

697. Sketches by Blight, taken in 1862 and 1863, of the Old Thatched Tavern, Greenhill Street, Stratford-on-Avon; cottages at Snitterfield; old houses in Chapel Street near New Place.

698. Shakespeare's Hall. An etching so entitled, showing the Town Hall, Chapel Street and the Guild Chapel, Stratford-on-Avon. Published by Ward, 1827.

699. Sketches by Blight, taken in 1863, of the Old Black Swan, river-side, and timbered houses in Greenhill Street, Stratford-on-Avon; an Elizabethan house at Tiddington, a hamlet in the parish of Alveston, Stratford-on-Avon; the roof of the ancient Chapel at the Manor-House, Shottery; old houses in the village of Charlecote.

700. Shakespeare's Birth-Place as it appeared at the time of the Jubilee. Fahey lithog. Published by J. Ward, 1827.

701. The Birth-Place of Shakespeare. London, published by O. Hodgson. An uncoloured view of the exterior. The house is represented as it appeared about the year 1812, but the engraving seems to be of a later date.

702. The Guildhall, Aston Cantlowe, J. Saunders, 1825.—Exterior of Shakespeare's Birth-Place, 1847, a sketch by Fairholt.—The King's Head Inn, Aylesbury, 1865, and the back of the White Swan in the Rother Market, Stratford-on-Avon, 1863, sketches by Blight. Another view by Fairholt of the exterior of the Birth-Place, 1847.

703. Charlecote House. Drawn by J. P. Neale. Engraved by W. Radclyffe, 1820.

704. Sketches, taken by Blight in 1863 and 1864, of an old timbered house at Charlecote; hood-mould termination, interior of the porch door, and door on south side of the Chancel of the Guild Chapel; Warkmore Bridge over the Stour, between Milcote and Weston, looking towards Stratford, the stream dividing the parishes of Old Stratford and Weston-on-Avon; an ancient fire-place in a room at the gateway of Charlecote House, with a water-colour view of the gateway itself.

705. Sketches by Blight of objects at the Guild Chapel, 1864,—handle of door on the south side of the Chancel; canopy of second panel from the tower, south side of nave; portions of wood-carving from an old screen; the doorway to the bell-loft, and interior of the north doorway.

706. Mary Arden's house, from a sketch by Saunders.

707. Sketches taken by Blight in 1863, one of Charlecote House, and another of its ancient stables; old houses at Shottery.—Shottery, 1848, from a sketch by F. Goodall, R.A.—Old timber from the Birth-Place, two sketches by Blight, 1864.—Anne Hathaway's Cottage, from a sketch by Fairholt.

708. Sketches by Blight, 1863, of small pieces of old timber from the Birth-Place; the back of Downing's house in Henley Street; backs of old houses in the High Street, Stratford-on-Avon; ancient fire-place at George's farm-house, Grendon Underwood.

709. Henley-in-Arden, a sketch by Fairholt, taken in 1854.

710. Sketches taken by Blight in 1863 and 1864 of Barton-on-the-Heath; Rother Street, Stratford-on-Avon; old cottage at Weston-on-Avon; timbered cottages near the Bell Lane, Snitterfield; old houses at Uxbridge; timbered buildings at Welford; the old rectory and barn, Clifford-Chambers; a view of Luddington; Snitterfield Church; timbered cottage near the Chapel Lane, Luddington; a lane in Snitterfield; interior of old house at Bishopton.

711. A large ground-plan of the Church and Churchyard at Stratford-on-Avon, taken about the year 1800.

712. View of the exterior of the Birth-Place, from a sketch taken in 1846. Drawn by J. T. Clark. Engraved by T. H. Ellis.

713. Anne Hathaway's Cottage, drawn from nature and on stone by J. Brandard, Leamington.

Published by C. Elston. This is an independent view taken from the road.

714. A portrait of Sir William Davenant, the poet's godson. Jo. Greenhill pinx. W. Faithorne sculp., 1673.—Front of the Crown Inn, Oxford, a sketch taken by Blight in July, 1864.

715. A perspective view of the New Place, the residence of Shakespeare, with the Chapel, Gild Hall and Alms Houses, with part of the Falcon Inn. John Jordan of Stratford del., 1793.—A view of part of Old Stratford from the Evesham road, dogs in the foreground, a sketch by Jordan, 1793. These are the original drawings from which the reduced copies in the Saunders collection were taken.

716. A large and curious plan by Jordan of Stratford-on-Avon and its neighbourhood, c. 1790. In the corners are inartistic views of the Church and Guild Chapel.

717. The "room in which Shakspere was born" and the exterior of the Birth-Place. The latter is a view similar to that in No. 561, but with several variations in the minor details. Two lithographs "drawn from nature on stone" by J. Brandard. Leamington, C. Elston.

718. Anne Hathaway's Cottage, an unfinished sketch taken by Blight in 1864.

719. A view of the Falcon Inn and Church Street, Stratford-on-Avon, by Captain Saunders.

720. A full-length portrait of James I. on his throne, with verses that have been attributed to Shakespeare. Simon Passæus sculpsit, London. John Bill excudit.

721. Miserere seats in the Chancel of Holy Trinity Church, Stratford-on-Avon, from original sketches by H. B. Clements.

722. Anne Hathaway's bed and the settle at her cottage, sketched by P. Dighton, 1834. The original drawing from which the published lithographs were taken.

723. Original tracings made by the elder Ireland, c. 1790, of the water-marks upon the paper on which Shakespeare's will is written.

724. A large view of the Guild Chapel, 1807.

725. Sketches taken by Blight in 1863 of Wixford, Hillborough and Broom.

726. The Chandos portrait of Shakespeare, a mezzotint engraved by Samuel Cousins, 1849.

727. Interior of Stratford Church. A sketch by Blight, 1864.

728. A coloured print, with a view of Shakespeare's monumental effigy and part of the Chancel of Stratford Church, as seen through an open door on the south.

729. The town of Pershore. Blight, 1865.

730. Interior of the old Crown Inn at Rochester; remains of the Roman Pharos and first Christian Church at Dover,—original sketches by F. W. Fairholt.—Shottery, from a sketch by the same.

731. "Front View of the Houses in Henley Street in Stratford, the reputed Birth-Place of the immortal Poet." Engraved on wood from an original sketch by Jordan. One of six copies only that were taken before the block was de-

stroyed. This is a small view showing the cottages on the west of the Birth-Place.

732. Wilmecote, from a sketch taken by Fairholt in 1852. Copied by Blight, 1864.

733. A volume of collections respecting the Birth-Place, consisting of the following pieces,—the exterior traced from a sketch taken by D. Parkes in July, 1806.—Printed hand-bill of an auction of the estate that was projected in March, 1805.—A large view of the exterior traced from an original sketch by Jordan that was destroyed in the lamentable fire which destroyed every vestige of the celebrated Staunton collection.—Sketches taken by Blight in 1864 of the kitchen and of the birth-room.—Pen-and-ink drawings of the exterior, the first from a photograph taken in 1858, and the other from one believed to be of about the same date.—Elevations of the house before the restoration was commenced, four large drawings.—Plan of the estate and adjoining properties by Joseph Hill, in two states of the plate. —The cellar, a sketch by Blight, 1864.—A coloured lithograph of a part of the town near the Birth-Place during the period of a jubilee, evidently for the most part fanciful.—The exterior, from a photograph taken by H. T. Buckle about the year 1854.—Another view, printed by M. and N. Hanhart, a lithograph by C. Graf.—The exterior, from the Mirror, January, 1823, with a slight variation from, and a lighter impression than, the one in No. 634, and another "from an old print," W. Harvey del., T. Williams sc., from the prospectus of the Birth-Place Committee, 1847.—The exterior, drawn by R. B. Wheler, engraved by F. Eginton, 1806; another, D.

Parkes del., 1806, J. Basire sculp.—An engraved copy of Greene's view of 1769, from Malone's Supplement, 1780.—" A House in Stratford-upon-Avon in which the famous poet Shakespeare was born," R. Greene del., B. Cole sculp., 1769.—A small clumsy water-colour sketch of old houses in Henley Street, 1820.—The exterior, a copy by Blight of a photograph taken soon after the removal of the adjoining houses.—The birth-room, a lithograph, c. 1840.—The kitchen, etch'd by S. Ireland, 1795.—An original pencil sketch of the exterior taken by J. P. Neale, 4 July, 1820.—The House in which Shakespeare was born, published by F. and G. Ward, Stratford, drawn and printed by G. Rowe.—The exterior, drawn and etched by W. Rider, published by J. Merridew, 1827.—Its appearance in 1806, R. B. Wheler delin., C. F. Green lithog., May, 1823.—Its appearance in 1824, C. F. Green delin. et lithog.—North and south parts of the chamber in which Shakespeare was born, C. F. Green delin. et lithog.—The shop, C. F. Green lithog., March, 1823.—The kitchen, C. F. Green delin. et lithog. —Arms of the Merchant of the Staple and the old sign affixed to Shakespeare's House.—David and Goliah, from the plaster-relievo formerly in the house of Shakespeare's birth, C. F. Green lithog.—The exterior, from a prospectus in which subscriptions were solicited for the restoration of the Church, 1835.—Engraved views of the exterior, both evidently taken from the sketch, No. 521, the first from the edition of Shakespeare that issued from the Chiswick Press in 1814, and the second, Alexander del., John Thompson sc., from Britton's Remarks on the Life and Writings of Shakespeare, 1818.—Three small engraved views of the exterior, from Clara Fisher's Shakespearean Cabinet, 1830.—A large engraving of the exterior from the Shakespeare Newspaper, 1847.—The exterior and the birth-room, large chromo-lithographs by Frederick Dangerfield from drawings made by S. Stanesby in 1856. These were amongst the last sketches of these objects that were made previously to the restoration, and they are extremely accurate.—Two other views of the exterior and the birth-room, coloured lithographs from drawings by Mrs. P. Dighton, published at Stratford-on-Avon, 1835.—Ireland's original view of the exterior, a water-colour sketch, slightly defective, taken by him in 1792, with the engraving from it that was published in 1795.—The exterior, from a sketch by Saunders, a privately issued lithograph.—The exterior, with the Swan and Maidenhead, a wood-engraving from the prospectus issued by the Birth-Place Committee in 1847, and therein stated to have been taken " from a recent drawing."—Two lithographic views of the exterior, without date or artists' names, as it appeared in 1769 and about 1840.

734. Painting of the Death of Becket on the west wall of the nave, south of the entrance to the Guild Chapel, Fisher del. Below are fragments of inscriptions not in the published copy.

735. The Exaltation of the Holy Cross, paintings on the south side of the chancel of the Guild Chapel. Fisher del.

736. Saint Modwena and St. Edmund the King, paintings in the westernmost niches on the south and north sides of the nave of the Guild Chapel. Fisher del.

737. Sketches of the north and south sides of the chancel of the Guild Chapel, showing the situation of the paintings; the paintings at the vicar's door. Fisher del.

738. An angel with admonitory verses, a painting on the west wall of the Guild Chapel, south of the entrance and beneath the Death of Becket. Fisher del.

739. Plan of Shakespeare's Birth-Place, W. Hemings delin., 1824. C. F. Green lithog.

740. Erthe onte of Erth ys wondurly wrought,— metrical inscriptions on the west wall of the nave of the Guild Chapel. These are the verses in No. 738, separately drawn by Fisher and on a larger scale.

741. A coloured map of Leicestershire, with a ground-plan of Leicester, and a delineation of the boundaries of "King Richards feild," from Speed's Theatre, 1610.

742. Original drawings by Mrs. P. Dighton, 1834, of the Falcon sign surrounded by presumed Shakespearean relics; Shakespeare's desk; the font and base of the market-cross; Luddington Chapel; interior of Anne Hathaway's Cottage; exterior of Stratford Church.

743. A coloured map of Kent, with plans of Canterbury and Rochester, from Speed, 1610.

744. A large printed hand-bill respecting a burglary at Charlecote House, 1850, with a list of the articles stolen.

745. A coloured map of Gloucestershire, with plans of Gloucester and Bristol. Speed, 1610.

746. A ground-plan of the Church and Churchyard of Stratford-on-Avon, executed about the year 1800.

747. A coloured map of Oxfordshire, with a plan of Oxford, 1605. From Speed, 1610.

748. A view of Oxford by Hoefnagle, 1574.

749. A large sketch of the mill and part of the mill-bridge, Stratford-on-Avon, taken about the year 1820.

750. M. William Shaks-peare, His True Chronicle Historie of the Life and Death of King Lear and his three Daughters,—a large fragment of the Pide Bull edition of 1608, with numerous textual variations.

751. Foole Vpon Foole, or Six Sortes of Sottes, shewing their hues, humours and behauiours, with their want of wit in their shew of wisdome. Not so strange as true. Written by one seeming to haue his mothers witte, when some say he is fild with his father's fopperie, and hopes he liues not without companie. Clonnico de Curtanio Snuffe. London, printed for William Ferbrand, dwelling neere Guild-hall gate ouer against the Maidenhead, 1600. Quarto.—No other copy of this, the first edition, is known to exist, and it differs importantly from the later ones. This extremely curious book, written by one of the poet's colleagues, is described in the Outlines of the Life of Shakespeare, ed. 1887, i. 322.

752. The most excellent Historie of the Merchant of Venice, printed by I. R. for Thomas Heyes, and are to be sold in Paules Church-yard at the signe of the Greene Dragon, 1600. Quarto.

The title-page and three leaves in facsimile. Malone's copy, presented to him by Dr. Farmer.

753. The Lives of the Noble Grecians and Romanes compared together by that grave learned Philosopher and Historiographer, Plutarke of Chœronea ; translated out of Greeke into French by Iames Amiot, and out of French into English by Thomas North. Imprinted at London by Richard Field for Bonham Norton, 1595. Folio. —There are sound reasons for believing that this is the edition that was used by Shakespeare.

754. A large collection of manuscript pieces in verse and prose, mostly of a comical nature, partly written and partly compiled by an Oxonian in the reign of Charles the First. It includes, at p. 74, Basse's verses, here entitled, "an Epitaph on Mr. Shakespeare," at pp. 119–121 verses on the play of Ignoramus, at p. 141 an allusion to the Globe Theatre ; at p. 232 lines of " Shakespeare on Sir John Coome." At pp. 182–217 is a contemporary transcript of the lost edition of Earle's Microcosmography, 1626, containing numerous textual variations and several passages omitted in the later impressions, e.g., the following in the Character of a Player,—"his commings in are tollerable, yet in smal money, and, like Halifax great vicaradge, most in twopences." 4to.

755. Birth-Place sketches by Blight, 1864,— the interior of the Record Room ; the room behind the shop ; the shop.

756.—The back of the Birth-Place, from a photograph taken previously to the restoration.

757. A chair formerly at Anne Hathaway's Cottage and called Shakespeare's Courting-Chair,

from Ireland's Views, 1795. Two copies of this wood-cut, varying slightly from each other.

758. Sketches taken by Blight in 1863 of interior of room on the ground-floor of the ancient house in the Rother Market, the church of Weston-on-Avon, and old houses at Shottery.

759. Deale Castle and the neighbouring sea-coast, W. Hollar delin.

760. Shakespeare's Birth-Place as it appeared previous to the Jubilee in 1769. C. F. Green lithog., 1823.

761. Upper room of the ancient house in the Rother Market. Blight, 1863.

762. Three engraved views of the exterior of the Birth-Place, the first drawn by Calvert, on stone by W. P. Sherlock, published by J. Ward; the second either engraved or drawn by Bonner; and the third marked as published by J. Boosey & Co., lithographers, 310, Strand. The last is slightly varied from, but is evidently a copy of, Fahey's lithograph of 1827.

763. London,—a diminutive view, with the theatres, in the title-page of the edition of the Bible published at Cambridge in 1648; a long narrow view showing the theatres and part of Southwark, c. 1640; a view of the sixteenth century, Londra, Fr. Valegio f.

764. The interior of an old English theatre, Sir John Falstaff and Mrs. Quickly in the foreground, from Kirkman's Witts or Sport upon Sport, 1672. This is the very rare original engraving, not the later copy so often substituted

for it. It is this engraving, not the book itself, that is of so much rarity.

765. The Church of Grendon Underwood, a sketch taken by Blight in 1865.

766. The Right Honourable and most noble Henry Wriothsley, Earle of Southampton, Baron of Titchfield, Knight of the most noble Order of the Garter. Simon Passæus sculp., 1617; are to be sould in Popes Head Ally by John Sudbury and Georg Humble.

767. South-east Prospect of Stratford-on-Avon, 1746.

768. The Market-Cross, Stratford-on-Avon, as it appeared in 1820. Drawn and lithographed by C. F. Green.

769. Stratford Bridge; Ireland, 1795.—Exterior of the Birth-Place, with small portions of the adjoining houses; Mason sc., 1825.—A view of Wilmecote, 1852.—Anne Hathaway's Cottage; Ireland, 1795.

770. Jubilee Amphitheatre, drawn by R. B. Wheler, engraved by F. Eginton, 1806.—The monumental effigy, C. Graf lith., published by F. & E. Ward, Stratford-on-Avon.

771. Charlecote House; Ireland, 1795.—New Place and the Guild Chapel, drawn from nature and on stone by J. Brandard, published by J. C. Elston, Leamington, lithographed by Day & Haghe.

772. The Church and Free-School, Hampton Lucy, 1822; Saunders del., C. F. Green lithog., 1824. An unpublished view.

773. Chapel of the Holy Cross, Stratford-on-Avon, showing the Grammar-School and site of New Place. Printed by M. & N. Hanhart. C. Graf lith., London. Published by Edward Adams.

774. New Place, Guild Chapel, &c. Ireland, 1795.

775. The Hall at Charlecote "where Shakespeare was tried." An uncoloured lithograph from a drawing by Mrs. P. Dighton, 1835.

776. Bidford, Warwickshire, and arms of the Merchant of the Staple in a pane of glass formerly in the Birth-Place. Ireland, 1795.

777. An original tracing made by the elder Ireland, c. 1790, of the signature of Shakespeare from a deed, in Mr. Wallis's hand, belonging to the Featherstonhaugh family.

778. Charlecote Hall and Stratford Church. W. Rider, Leamington, July 1st, 1835.

779. Back of George's Farm; J. Niemann, 1847.—David and Goliah; Ireland, 1795.—George's Farm, formerly the Ship, Grendon Underwood, 1847.

780. The Ancient Chapel of Bishopton, its font and piscina. An original drawing, c. 1810.—A sketch by Fairholt of the Lich-gate, Welford Church, c. 1847.

781. The Birth-Place of Shakespeare, a coloured view published by O. Hodgson.—View of the Brook House "in which Shakespeare was really born," J. Jordan del., 1799

782. A view of Chapel Street, showing the old character of the house on the New Place side of the Town-Hall. Drawn and engraved by T. Radclyffe, 1829.

783. The monumental effigy, the grave-stone and entrance to Charnel-House. Ireland, 1795.

784. Arms in the windows of Stratford Church; arms in the window and porch of the Guild Chapel. Dugdale, 1656.

785. A view of Stratford-on-Avon from the bridge. Drawn and engraved by T. Radclyffe, 1829.

786. A lower room at the Birth-Place, and the garret over the birth-room, 1852.—Exterior of the Birth-Place, Ph. de la Motte, 1788.

787. The Nag's Head Inn, Bicester, sketched by Blight in 1865.—Plan of Shakespeare's close.

788. Exterior of Anne Hathaway's Cottage. Barn on the left, but differing from the view by Rider. A drawing in water-colours executed about the year 1830.

789. Monument in Stratford Church to the memory of the Earl and Countess of Totness. Dugdale, 1656.

790. Anne Hathaway's Cottage, a wood-engraving from the Casket of 23 April, 1837.—Arms in Snitterfield Church, from Dugdale, 1656.—Exterior of Stratford Church, Fahey lithog., published by J. Ward.—Interior of Stratford Church, T. G. Flowers, Edinburgh.—Herne's Oak, from the Mirror of 15 July, 1826.—Sign of the Boar's Head Tavern, 1668.

791. Shakespeare's School and Old Guildhall. London, J. Harwood, 1847.—Views of Stratford-on-Avon and the College, drawn by R. B. Wheler, engraved by F. Eginton, 1806.—Clopton House, from Ireland's Views, 1795.

792. Interior of Anne Hathaway's Cottage. An uncoloured lithograph from a drawing by Mrs. P. Dighton, 1835.

793. The Birth-Room, from a drawing by J. Brandard. A proof before letters.

794. Anne Hathaway's Bed and Chair. An uncoloured lithograph from a drawing by Mrs. P. Dighton, 1835.

795. The Deer-Barn at Grove Field, Warwickshire, drawn by W. Jackson, 1798. A lithograph.

796. The monumental effigy, a coloured view published, although not so stated, by C. Elston of Leamington. Probably a proof before letters.

797. Bidford Grange. Ireland, 1795.

798. Front of Charlecote House. Allan E. Everitt del. M. & N. Hanhart imp. J. Brandard lith. Published by H. T. Cooke, Warwick.

799. The Exterior of the Birth-Place from a drawing by J. Brandard. Shows part of the Swan and Maidenhead. Four figures opposite the shop-window.

800. Shakespeare's Desk. A coloured lithograph from a drawing by Mrs. P. Dighton, 1835.

801. Exterior of Stratford Church, Fahee lithog., published by J. Ward.—A view of the Church from the opposite side of the river, printed

by M. & N. Hanhart, C. Graf lith., published by Edward Adams.

802. Some Account of the Life of Mr. William Shakespeare. By N. Rowe. From the 1709 edition of the Poet's works. 8vo.

803. Englands Helicon. At London, printed by J. R. for Iohn Flasket, and are to be sold in Paules Church-yard at the signe of the Beare, 1600. Quarto.—The present copy of this extremely rare book unfortunately wants a few leaves, but it is complete in all the Shakespearean pieces.

804. Sir Thomas Smithes Voiage and Entertainment in Rushia, with the tragicall ends of two Emperors and one Empresse within one Moneth during his being there. Printed at London for Nathanyell Butter, 1605.—Quarto. The curious allusion to the old tragedy of Hamlet is at sig. K

805. An oblong volume, in manuscript, that belonged to one Giles Lodge in 1591, containing the original music to a number of songs and dances, including several that are either quoted or mentioned by Shakespeare, and no doubt familiarly known to him, e.g., Robin Hoode, a galiarde, passa mesers galiarde, the antycke, a pavion, a hornepippe, the passe a mesures pavion, a round, the hunt ys uppe, a dumpe, quarter brawles, the Frenche galiarde, all of grene willowe, and a measure. Amongst the miscellaneous pieces may be mentioned Westones pavion and "my Lord of Essex songe," the latter being thus noted, *finis quoth William Hewese.* So Tyrwhitt's conjecture respecting the W. H. of the Sonnets may thus receive a trifling support. At

the end of the book, following a collection of receipts, is an unpublished drama in five acts, avowedly written for boy-actors, and entitled "a new comody of July and Julian." There is no date to this curious production, but it may be confidently assigned to the period of Shakespeare's boyhood.

NOTES.

Page 6, line 7. More difficult to obtain. The market has been swept and the day has now gone by for reasonable expectations to rise beyond the endless acquisition of modern Shakespeareana and the occasional gleaning of an important rarity. So it was with no small amusement that those who are conversant with such matters observed the alarm that was expressed by more than one journal at a recent movement which was supposed to involve the danger of the Shakespearean interests of London being sacrificed to those of Warwickshire. Perhaps the worthy critics imagined that the dulcet tones of a committee of solicitation would attract early editions and title-deeds from the firmament,—it is difficult to understand how else they could be gathered to an extent that would allure metropolitan students to the bank of the Avon. At the same time it is only fair to recognise the local utility of the collection that is now being formed in the elegant library which Stratford owes to the generous liberality of Mr. Charles Flower.

Page 6, line 8. An impenetrable fifty-thousand volume library.—It may be well, in view of the present tendency to herald numerical supremacy as a test of value, to observe that no ambition of the kind has stimulated the gathering of the collection which is described in the preceding pages. The whole, indeed, is comprised in about two hundred volumes, a striking contrast to the seven thousand that are already accumulated in the recently-formed Shakespearean Library at Birmingham; but victory in these cases is not always with the largest battalions, and the accomplished Shakespearean Director of that town, Mr. Sam. Timmins, would be the first to acknowledge that at least fifty per cent. of its modern acquisitions could be consigned to the waste-paper basket without the slightest prejudice to the interests of literature or to the honour of the great dramatist. I speak feelingly, in the hope that the Shakespeare drag-net may be relieved of its weeds and sand, for if a much larger percentage of my own writings in this kind could be eliminated, the operation would add very much to my complacency. Perhaps, however, in my own individual case, it is better as it is ;—" our virtues might be proud, if our faults whipped them not."

Page 7, line 22. New Place.—The ancient title-deeds of New Place, which form so distinguished a feature of the present collection, were discovered two years ago by Mr. Richard Sims, of the British Museum, in the private archives of Wallop Hall, co. Salop. The discovery of these indentures has added little or nothing of moment to our previous knowledge of the history of the estate, but they are inestimable as personal relics of the great dramatist. Ancient deeds are almost the only articles that, with proper care, maintain their precise original condition for indefinite periods.

Page 9, line 20. The present one.—Nearly the whole of the drawings and engravings have been mounted with great taste and judgment by Mr. James Biddle, of North Street, Brighton, and so mounted that they are protected from the danger that would have accrued had they been liable to contact with other surfaces.

INDEX.

Abington Abbey, 498
Accolti, Bernard, 90.
Acton, 464.
Adams, Edward, 370, 547, 773, 801.
Adderbury, 451.
Agar, I. S., 272.
Albans. See *Saint Albans*.
Alcazar, battle of, 18.
Alexander, W., 625, 733.
Allot, Robert, 283.
All's Well that Ends Well, 40, 90.
Alms'-houses, 715.
Alne, Little, 437.
Alveston, 602, 638.
Anne Hathaway's Cottage, 210, 282, 289.—*Exterior*, 317, 403, 547, 558, 636, 639, 677, 691, 707, 713, 718, 769, 788, 790.—*Interior*, 319, 321, 348, 372, 494, 496, 498, 511, 515, 568, 677, 680, 742, 792. —*Relics*, 499, 502, 722, 757, 794. —*The well*, 319.
Anton, Robert, 191.
Antony and Cleopatra, 103.
Archer, J., 614.
Armin, Robert, 32, 751.
Aston Cantlowe, 642, 643, 644. 653, 691, 702.
As You Like It, 20, 34, 35, 110.
Atherston-upon-Stour, 592.
Austin, Samuel, 92.
Aylesbury, 267, 702.
Baker, Alfred, 552.
Baker, Sir Richard, 241.
Banbury, 440, 464.
Bancroft, Thomas, 155.
Bandello, Matteo, 100.
Barber, J. V., 268.
Barcheston, 671.
Barclay, Sir Richard, 181.
Barlichway Hundred, 350, 365.
Barnstaple, 215.
Bartholomew Fair, 216.
Barton, 467.

Barton-on-the-Heath, 447, 538, 672. 710.
Basire, J., 733.
Basse, William, 754.
Bath, plan of, 232.
Baynard's Castle, 590.
Beaconsfield, 475, 565.
Bearley, 519, 643, 672.
Bear Tavern, 250.
Bedell, Gabriel, 201.
Bedfordshire, 301.
Beighton, Henry, 326, 333, 350.
Bell, J., 601.
Bennet, Thomas, 216.
Berkshire, 299, 301, 308.
Bible in Stratford Church, 424.
Bicester, 787.
Bidford, 472, 475, 536, 742, 776, 797.
Billesley, 576.
Birmingham, 688.
Birth of Merlin, 22.
Birth-Place, 81, 102, 111, 112, 123, 348, 733, 739.—*Exterior*, 362, 455, 491, 493, 505, 507, 521, 525, 530, 548, 551, 552, 556, 559, 561, 570, 573, 574, 575, 577, 581, 584, 600, 601, 608, 613, 614, 615, 624, 625, 627, 634, 637, 646, 652, 654, 668, 675, 678, 679, 695, 700, 701, 702, 712, 717, 731, 733, 760, 762, 769, 781, 786, 799.—*Interior*, 303, 455, 491, 493, 494, 498, 502, 505, 507, 508, 518, 522, 526, 530, 667, 683, 733, 755, 786.—*Relics*, 349, 496, 522, 526, 581, 594, 596, 598, 647, 649, 651, 688, 691, 707, 708, 776.
Birth-Place Committee, 733.
Birth-Room, 322, 362, 505, 510, 526, 530, 549, 571, 631, 685, 717, 733, 793.
Bishopton, 588, 599, 606, 612, 642, 657, 685, 690, 691, 710, 780.

Blackfriars Estate, 124, 148, 149, 165, 208.
Blackfriars Theatre, 198.
Blome, Richard, 242.
Blore, E., 659.
Blurt, Master Constable, 230.
Boaden, John, 387.
Boaistuau, Pierre, 100.
Boars' Head Tavern, 790.
Bodenham, John, 44, 803.
Bonner, 762.
Boosey & Co., 762.
Bott, William, 226.
Bottom the Weaver, 54.
Bracebridge, Mrs., 638.
Braithwait, Richard, 201.
Brandard, J., 561, 566, 571, 661, 713, 717, 771, 793, 798, 799.
Braun, 239, 313, 315, 438, 529.
Brent Brook, 416.
Brentford, 340, 472.
Bridge, Stratford, 441, 489, 516, 769.
Bridge Street, Stratford-on-Avon, 441, 489, 567, 689.
Bristol, 745.
Britton, John, 733.
Brome, Richard, 201.
Brook House, 781.
Broom, co. Warwick, 406, 725.
Brulovis, Caspar, 164.
Buckinghamshire, 301.
Buckler, J. C., 297, 484.
Bullock, G., 389.
Burmington, 462.
Burton, Robert, 273.
Butcher, William, 270, 353.
Calvert, 762.
Cambridgeshire, 301.
Camden, William, 75, 189, 253, 357.
Campden House, 395.
Camus, John Peter, 187.
Canterbury, 377, 438, 743.
Carew, Lord and Lady, 264.
Cartwright, William, 230.
Casket, the, 613, 790.
Cawdray, Robert, 230.
Chandos Portrait, 726.
Chapel Lane, Stratford-on-Avon, 393.
Chapel Street, Stratford-on-Avon, 677, 697, 698, 782.
Chapel Street House, once Hathaway's, 163, 170, 195, 213, 218, 250.

Chapman, George, 201.
Chapman, Philip, 70.
Chapman & Hall, 318, 356.
Charlecote Church, 305, 581, 589, 621.
Charlecote Gate-house, 518, 685, 689, 704. This building is included in some of the views of the exterior.
Charlecote House.—*Exterior*, 268, 269, 318, 328, 333, 371, 413, 497, 566, 610, 640, 655, 677, 685, 696, 703, 707, 771, 778, 798.—*Interior*, 335, 348, 356, 775.—*Relics*, 320, 744.
Charlecote Traditions, 257.
Charlecote Village, 635, 699, 704.
Charnel House, 306, 320, 366, 468, 477, 591, 681, 783.
Chettle, Henry, 51, 178.
Chiswick Press, 733.
Church Restoration Fund, 733.
Church, Stratford, 216, 225, 248, 366, 453, 454, 711, 746, 784.—*Exterior*, 271, 286, 296, 297, 298, 300, 319, 358, 392, 396, 414, 426, 432, 434, 444, 450, 469, 482, 484, 513, 514, 554, 565, 596, 609, 716, 742, 778, 790, 801.—*Interior*, 266, 286, 306, 370, 427, 429, 430, 432, 433, 434, 436, 439, 446, 459, 468, 469, 477, 481, 482, 484, 486, 487, 581, 727, 728, 790.—See *Clopton Chapel* and *Saint Thomas's Chapel*.
Church Street, Stratford-on-Avon, 492, 648, 651, 658, 673, 695, 719.
Churchyard, Stratford, 431, 711, 746.
Cinthio, Giraldi, 91.
Clark, J. T., 712.
Clarke, John, 157.
Clements, H. B., 550, 721.
Clifford Chambers, 612, 671, 693, 710.
Clopton, Anne, 466.
Clopton Chapel, 390, 427, 452, 454, 456, 626.
Clopton common-lands, 224.
Clopton estate, 1, 223.
Clopton family, 1.
Clopton House, 1, 663, 791.
Clopton, William, 139, 226, 466.
Cock-and-Pye tavern, 689.
Cokain, Francis, 230.

Cole, B., 733.
Colin Clout, 48.
College, Stratford, 221, 345, 499, 605, 617, 623, 630, 644, 673, 791.
Collier, W., 324, 332.
Collins, Francis, 141, 214.
Collins, Thomas, 201.
Combe, John, 136, 278, 662, 674, 754.
Combe, Thomas, 147.
Comical Gallant, 89.
Cooke, H. T., 661, 798.
Cordy, John, 272.
Cornelianum Dolium, 95.
Cornwal, 215.
Cornwallis, Sir William, 279.
Cotgrave, John, 160.
Council-Chamber, Stratford-on-Avon, 349, 550, 647, 649.
Court, William, 227, 228.
Court-Leet Books, 67, 68.
Cousins, Samuel, 726.
Coventry, 312.
Cox, Rev. Thomas, 400, 465.
Crab-tree, Shakespeare's, 175, 368, 369, 407, 457, 480, 523.
Cranley, Thomas, 201.
Cromwell, Thomas, Lord, 49.
Cross-on-the-Hill, 228, 578.
Daisy Hill, 633, 640, 655, 795.
Danckerts, Dancker, 244.
Dangerfield, Frederick, 733.
Datchet, 474.
Davenant, Sir William, 216, 714.
David and Goliah, 512, 779.
Davies, John, 30.
Day & Haghe, 581, 638.
Day & Son, 421.
Day, Matthew, 52.
Deal Castle, 759.
Dean, T. A., 384.
Decker, Thomas, 52, 59, 201.
Deddington, 464.
Deer-Barn, 795.
De la Motte, 786.
Deloney, Thomas, 40.
Denmark, the King of, 15.
Dennis, John, 89.
Derbyshire, 301.
Desk, Shakespeare's, 526, 562, 694, 742, 800.
Destruction of Troy, 38, 72.
Devonshire, 215.
Dewint, P., 358, 360, 635.
Dighton, Mrs. P., 296, 302, 322, 335, 344, 362, 382, 403, 412, 556, 558, 562, 722, 733, 742, 775, 792, 794, 800.
Dingles, the, 643.
Doddridge, Justice, 156.
Dorastus and Fawnia, 94.
Dorsetshire, 215.
Dover, 316, 440, 485, 730. See *Shakespeare's Cliff*.
Downes, John, 61.
Drayton, Michael, 104, 230.
Droeshout. See *Portraits*.
Drury-Lane Theatre, 122.
Dryden, John, 84, 117, 229.
Dugdale, Sir William, 295, 363, 365, 375, 466, 535, 784, 789, 790.
Earle, John, 754.
Earthquake in London, 132, 280.
Eastward Hoe, 201.
Edward the Third, 27.
Eginton, F., 7, 388, 441, 450, 733, 770, 791.
Ellis, T. H., 712.
Elm, the Boundary, 222.
Elston, C., 561, 566, 713, 717, 796.
Elston, J. C., 771.
Ely Street, Stratford-on-Avon, 651.
England's Helicon, 803.
England's Parnassus, 283.
Epitia Tragedia, 91.
Essex, 299, 301, 308.
Essex, Earl of, 83, 230, 249, 394.
Eton, 324, 330, 475.
Euphues Golden Legacie, 110.
Everitt, Allen E., 661, 798.
Every Man in his Humour, 50.
Every Man out of his Humour, 201.
Exhall, 306.
Fahee, 694, 801.
Fahey, 700, 790.
Faire Em, 183.
Fairholt, F. W., 81, 380, 401, 665.
Falcon Tavern, Southwark, 247.
Falcon Tavern, Stratford-on-Avon, 206, 421, 719.
Field, John, 281.
Field, Nathaniel, 184.
Finden, W., 614.
Fisher, Clara, 733.
Fisher, Thomas, 290, 541 to 546, 734 to 738, 740.
Fitzook, H., 679.
Fleming, Abraham, 280.
Fletcher, John, 64.
Fletcher, Mrs., 398.

Florio, John, 666.
Flowers, T. G., 624, 631, 790.
Font, Shakespeare's, 286, 302, 412, 427, 742.
Free-School See *Grammar-School*.
Frith, Mary, 620.
Fulwood, Robert, 142.
Garden of the Muses, 44.
Gastrell, the Rev. Francis, 6.
Gayton, Edmund, 251.
Gaywood, Robert, 583.
Gee, John, 82.
George-and-Dragon Inn, 689.
Gibbs, Thomas, 78, 79.
Gilbirson, William, 36.
Glamorganshire, 215.
Globe Theatre, 245, 754.
Gloucester, 667, 745.
Gloucestershire, 215, 301, 745.
Golden Lion Inn, 591.
Golding, Arthur, 12.
Gonzaga, Curtio, 174.
Gosson, Stephen, 285.
Goulart, John, 230.
Graf, C., 370, 547, 551, 733, 770, 773, 801.
Grammar-School, 2, 29, 74, 341, 349, 504, 508, 550, 647, 651, 689, 773, 791.
Gray's Inn Hall, 582.
Green, C. F., 327, 457, 499. 609, 639, 733, 739, 760, 768, 772.
Greene, John, 134.
Greene, the Rev. Joseph, 2, 5, 42, 114, 216, 257, 282, 289, 426.
Greene, Richard, 298, 366, 396, 513, 588, 592, 602, 654, 733.
Greene, Robert, 94, 159.
Greene, Thomas, 137.
Greenhill Street, Stratford-on-Avon, 671, 684, 697, 699.
Greenwich Palace, 329.
Grendon Underwood, 267, 470, 475, 673, 708, 765, 779.
Grevin, Jaques, 97.
Griffith, Sir George, 466.
Grimmitt, Richard, 5.
Groto, Luigi, 119.
Guild Chapel, 290, 319, 449, 487, 541, to 545, 581, 585, 594, 597, 598, 604, 628, 645, 647, 651, 656, 664, 688, 698, 704, 705, 734 to 738, 740, 784.—*Exterior*, 7, 349, 421, 715, 716, 724, 771, 773, 774.
Guild-Hall, Stratford, 7, 550, 715, 791.

Gwin, J., 426.
Hadriana Tragedia, 119.
Hall, John, 163, 176, 195, 616, 682.
Hamlet, 62, 101.
Hampton Lucy, 360, 643, 772.
Hanhart, M. & N., 370, 457, 570, 733, 798, 801.
Harding, E., 419.
Harding, J. D., 269.
Harding, S., 662.
Harington's Ariosto, 216.
Harrison, Stephen, 292.
Harsnet, Samuel, 47, 73.
Hart family, 123, 656.
Hart, Shakespeare, 152, 207.
Hartley, William, 56.
Harvey, Gabriel, 93.
Harvey, W., 733.
Harwood, J., 675, 791.
Hathaway, Anne, 353. See *Anne Hathaway's Cottage*.
Hathaway, Edmund, 194, 248.
Hathaway, Jane, 168, 169.
Hathaway, John, 199, 200, 252.
Hathaway, Richard, 204.
Hathaway, Robert, 203, 252, 254, 255.
Hathaway, Sarah, 255.
Hathaway, Susanna, 166, 195, 213.
Hathaway, Thomas, 163, 168, 169, 170, 195, 218, 250.
Heliodorus, 179.
Help to Discourse, 201.
Hemings, W., 739.
Henley-in-Arden, 496, 503, 667, 709.
Henley Street, Stratford-on-Avon, 348, 499, 575, 577, 611, 625, 646, 651, 660, 675, 684, 708, 733.—*Deeds*, 206, 210.
Henry the Fourth, 19, 26, 206.
Henry the Sixth, 9, 53.
Herne's Oak. See *Windsor*.
Hertfordshire, 301.
Heywood, Thomas, 14, 211.
Hickes, R., 444.
Higford, Henry, 26.
High Street, Stratford-on-Avon, 327, 397, 512, 520, 581, 611, 650, 656, 665, 685, 708.
Hill, Joseph, 733.
Hill, Richard, 225.
Hillborough, 725.
Hillingdon, 435, 524.
Historical Dictionary, 216.
Hodgson, O., 701, 781.

Hoefnagle, George, 339, 748.
Hoffman, a tragedy, 178.
Hole, William, 666.
Holland, Henry, 394, 555.
Hollands Leaguer, 41.
Hollar, 215, 242, 291, 299, 301, 316, 336, 338, 343, 346, 347, 363, 373, 374, 376, 417, 485, 509, 517, 532, 593, 595, 669, 759.
Honor of Armes, 34.
Hooper, S., 410.
Howell, James, 533.
Hullmandel, C., 694.
Hulme F. W., 318, 355.
Hundred Mery Talys, 196.
Hunsdon, Lord, 171.
Huntingdonshire, 301.
Hutchinson, H., 266.
Inganni comedia, 158, 174.
Ingannati comedia, 173.
Ireland forgeries, 60.
Ireland, Samuel, 364, 414, 442, 480, 633, 723, 733, 757, 769, 771, 774, 776, 777, 779, 783, 791, 797.
Irving, Washington, 348, 627.
Isle of Wight, 24, 299, 308.
Islip, co. Oxon, 310, 354, 423, 451.
Jackson, J. G., 318, 356.
Jackson, W., 795.
Jago, the Rev. Richard, 406.
James the First, 292, 720.
Jew of Malta, 180.
Johnson, John, 421.
Jones, Richard, 34.
Jones, the Rev. William, 24.
Jonson, Ben, 50, 108, 201, 210, 211, 216, 314, 383.
Jordan, John, 106, 175, 276, 355, 405, 410, 523, 715, 716, 731, 781.
Jubilee, the Stratford, 442, 521, 770.
Julius Cæsar, 97, 105, 118, 164, 277.
July and Julian, 805.
Keeper's Lodge, Fulbrooke, 640. See *Daisy Hill.*
Kenilworth Castle, 23, 535.
Kent, 299, 308, 316, 743.
King, D., 527.
Kingswood, co. Warwick, 246.
Kip, I., 330, 331.
Kip, William, 292, 351.
Kirkall, E., 333.
Kirkman, Francis, 230, 764.
Knolle Manor, 116.

Knyff, L., 330, 331.
Laing, C. D., 665.
Lambeth, 509.
Laneham, Robert, 23.
Langbaine, Gerard, 274.
Lapworth, co. Warwick, 167, 246, 251.
Lawford, George, 272.
Lear, King, 39, 47, 73, 193, 750.
Leicestershire, 301, 741.
Lightholder, Timothy, 396.
Lily, William, 29, 74.
Lincolns Inn Fields Theatre, 122.
Lincolnshire, 301.
Linton, W. J., 637, 680.
Lintott, Bernard, 192.
Lisbon nunnery, 188.
Little Alne, 437.
Lodge, Thomas, 110, 285.
Lombart, P., 293.
London,—*Bridge*, 238.—*Plans*, 239, 242, 313, 315, 529, 531, 539, 540.—*Views*, 162, 240, 241, 243, 244, 292, 376, 527, 532, 533, 555, 593, 763.
Long Lane, 693.
Lover's Complaint, 76.
Love's Labour's Lost, 21, 33.
Lucrece, Rape of, 4.
Lucy, Lady, 70, 98, 688.
Lucy, Sir Thomas, 70, 133, 257, 258, 259, 291, 293, 385, 500, 688.
Luddington, 320, 710, 742.
Macbeth, 87, 233.
Maces, the Stratford, 647, 689.
Malcontent, 58.
Malone, Edmund, 733.
Manuscript Miscellanies, 52, 277, 278.
Market-Cross, Stratford-on-Avon, 286, 327, 499, 632, 742, 788.
Marlowe, Christopher, 180, 287.
Marsh Gibbon, 671.
Marston, 467, 475.
Marston, John, 58, 201, 230.
Mason, 769.
Massuccio Salernitano, 154.
Mathews, Sir Tobie, 201.
Measure for Measure, 25, 91, 185, 277.
Medland, 419.
Meer Street, Stratford-on-Avon, 651.
Merchant of Venice, 8, 65, 752.
Mercutio, 84.
Meres, Francis, 17.

L

Merian, Matthew, 532.
Merlin, Birth of, 22.
Merridew, Henry, 7, 608.
Merridew, J., 733.
Merry Devil of Edmonton, 57, 107.
Merry Wives of Windsor, 89, 93.
Messalina, 603.
Microcosmos, 30.
Middle-Row, Stratford-on-Avon, 311, 567.
Middlesex, 299, 308, 352, 357, 361, 378.
Middle Temple, 518, 520, 534, 641, 670.
Middleton, Thomas, 230.
Midsummer Night's Dream, 54.
Milcote, 671.
Mill-Bridge, 490, 493, 495, 508, 554, 578, 607, 749.
Mill-Lane, 528.
Mill, Stratford, 414, 658, 749.
Mirror, The, 615, 634, 733, 790.
Miserere Stalls, 439, 472, 721.
Mitre Tavern, London, 237.
Moll, H., 367.
Moll Cutpurse, 620.
Monmouthshire, 215.
Monthly Magazine, 634.
Monumental Effigy, 42, 270, 272, 295, 334, 344, 380, 382, 384, 386 to 389, 659, 728, 770, 783, 796.
Morley, Thomas, 20.
Mortlake, 586.
Mount Tabor, 284.
Mucedorus, 71, 186.
Much Ado about Nothing, 28.
Mulberry-tree, 79, 80, 197.
Music, ancient, 805.
Musical Companion, 210, 230.
Naps upon Parnassus, 92.
Nash's House, 319, 325.
Nash, Thomas, 16, 201.
Neale, J. P., 286, 703, 733.
Neele, 257.
Newman, A., 421.
New Place, 1, 5, 6, 7, 125 to 131, 139, 140, 143 to 146, 151, 163, 195, 213, 325, 580, 715, 771, 773, 774.
Niemann, J., 779.
Nixon, the Rev. R., 694.
Nominal Orthography, 205.
Norden, John, 238, 352, 357, 361, 378, 539, 540, 560.
Norfolk, 301.
North, Thomas, 753.

Northamptonshire, 301.
Norwich, 563.
Nottinghamshire, 301.
Ogilby, John, 307.
Old Black Swan, 699.
Oldcastle, Sir John, 10.
Old Town, Stratford-on-Avon, 616, 682.
Oldys, William, 274.
Orthography, nominal, 205.
Othello, 42, 120.
Overton, Henry, 361.
Overton, John, 531.
Ovid, 12.
Oxford, 212, 359, 448, 451, 458, 464, 714, 747, 748.
Oxfordshire, 301, 747.
Packwood, co. Warwick, 217, 246.
Page, Anne, 373.
Palace of Pleasure, 201, 230.
Paris Garden, 281.
Parkes, D., 733.
Paroemiologia Anglo-Latina, 157.
Parris, E. T., 549.
Passe, Simon, 720.
Passionate Pilgrim, 14, 76, 99.
Pathlow Hill, 693.
Pauls. See *Saint Pauls*.
Paul's Cross, 236.
Payton, John, 111.
Peak, J., 586.
Pebworth, 475.
Peele, George, 18.
Pembrokeshire, 215.
Pendragon, 216.
Pericles, 46, 63, 108, 277.
Perkes, Thomas, 262.
Pershore, 464, 475, 729.
Peyto, Richard de, 223.
Phillips, Joseph, 206.
Phillips, Thomas, 389.
Pierce Penilesse, 16, 201.
Pipe, Richard, 52.
Plautus, 177.
Play-bill, 229.
Playford, John, 210, 230.
Pleasant Willy, 3, 43.
Plutarch, 753.
Poems, Shakespeare's, 31, 192, 211, 237.
Polimanteia, 257.
Portraits of Shakespeare, 31, 36, 69, 219, 220, 234, 235, 288, 334, 379, 391, 583, 726.
Postcombe, 462.
Promos and Cassandra, 25.

Prompt-copies, 233, 287.
Pulpit presented to Stratford-on-Avon Church by John Hall, 569.
Puritan, a comedy, 211.
Quiney, Richard, 206, 673.
Radclyffe, T., 640, 782, 785.
Radclyffe, W., 266, 268, 269, 358, 360, 635, 703.
Randolph, Thomas, 52, 95, 108, 230.
Record Box, 647.
Register, Stratford-on-Avon, 289, 424, 445.
Return from Parnassus, 37, 66, 201.
Rex Platonicus, 113.
Rice, Francis ap., 83.
Richards, N., 603.
Richardson, John, 251.
Richard the Second, 13.
Richmond Palace, 418.
Rider, W., 317, 321, 413, 640, 733, 778.
Ring, Shakespeare's, 688.
Roberts, Henry, 15.
Robinson, Thomas, 188.
Roche, Walter, 153.
Rochester, 381, 404, 422, 478, 482, 537, 564, 606, 730, 743.
Rocque, J., 323.
Roe, J., 610.
Rogers, 497, 516.
Romeo and Juliet, 45, 100.
Rooke, Hayman, 420.
Roscius Anglicanus, 61.
Rother Market, 581, 622, 651, 677, 685, 702, 710, 758, 761.
Rowe, G., 548.
Rowe, John, 71.
Rowe, Nicholas, 257, 282, 334, 802.
Rowley, William, 22.
Roxana, 629.
Rutlandshire, 301.
Rye, co. Sussex, 316.
Saint Albans, 476.
Saint Pauls, 517.
Saint Saviour's, Southwark, 553, 669.
Saint Thomas's Chapel, 428, 434, 487.
Sandells, Fulke, 194.
Satiro-Mastix, 59, 201.
Saunders, Captain, 686, 733, 772.
Saviolo, Vincentio, 35.
Saviours. See *Saint Saviour's*.
Saxton, Christopher, 309, 351.
Scarron, Paul, 230, 231.

School, Stratford-on-Avon. *Grammar School*.
Scriven, E., 387.
Segar, Sir William, 34.
Shakespeare, Anne, 206.
Shakespeare families, 115, 116, 167, 172, 217, 246, 289.
Shakespeare, John, 111, 142, 276.
Shakespeare Newspaper, 733.
Shakespeare's autograph, 777.
Shakespeare's Cliff, 337, 374, 401, 564, 595.
Shakespeare's Close, 787.
Shakespeare's Hall. See *Town-Hall*.
Shakespeare the Shoemaker, 210.
Sharp, John, 530.
Sharp, Thomas, 6, 78, 80.
Sharpe, Lewis, 230.
Shepherd, George, 668.
Sheppard, Samuel, 96, 201.
Sherlock, W. P., 762.
Sherwood & Co., 610.
Shirley, James, 121.
Shottery, 409, 501, 581, 651, 657, 671, 676, 677, 682, 683, 691, 699, 707, 730, 758.
Shrewley, co. Warwick, 172.
Shrewsbury, 294.
Silvayn, Alexander, 86.
Smith, A., 601.
Smithe, Sir Thomas, 230, 804.
Smythe, William, 226.
Snitterfield, 182, 262, 643, 661, 683, 690, 697, 710, 790.
Somersetshire, 215.
Somner, William, 377.
Sonnets, Shakespeare's, 277.
Southampton, Earl of, 24, 83, 150, 766.
Southamptonshire, 299, 308.
Speed, John, 232, 243, 294, 312, 361, 540, 741, 743, 745, 747.
Spenser, Edmund, 3, 43, 48.
Squeal of Cotswold, 260.
Stafford, John, 36.
Stanesby, S., 733.
Starter, Jan Jensen, 28.
Steeple Aston, 464.
Stent, P., 309, 316.
Stocks, the Stratford, 649.
Stokenchurch, 448.
Storer, J., 600.
Storer, J. & H. S., 610.
Straparola, Francesco, 93.
Stratford-on-Avon.—*Earliest guide*.

L. 2

book, 275.—*Levies*, 248.—*Plans*, 221, 261, 263, 265, 355, 580, 716, 746.—*Presentments*, 67, 68, 222. —*Views*, 488, 506, 619, 715, 767, 785, 791.
Stratton Audley, 470.
Stroude, William, 108.
Stukeley, William, 440, 579.
Sturley, Abraham, 135, 138, 228, 256.
Suckling, Sir John, 230.
Suffolk, 301.
Surrey, 299, 308.
Sussex, 299, 308.
Sutton, Robert, 56.
Swan, John, 201.
Swan Inn, Stratford-on-Avon, 111.
Swanwick, W. R., 263.
Sword of State, 572.
Symonson, Philip, 316.
Tailor, Robert, 109, 201.
Taming of the Shrew, 11.
Tarlton, Richard, 3.
Taylor, John, 161.
Tempest, 88, 210, 264, 687.
Temple Grafton, 467, 475.
Tetsworth, 448, 479.
Theatre, The, Shoreditch, 56.
Thomas. See *Saint Thomas.*
Thompson, John, 659, 733.
Thornton, T., 419.
Three Looks over London, 236.
Three Pigeons Inn, 448.
Tiddington, 699.
Timbre de Cardone, 28.
Titus Andronicus, 77, 85.
Tolley, J., 263.
Tombstone, Shakespeare's, 270, 295, 686, 783.
Tom Drum, 40.
Toms, W. H., 553.
Totness monument, 789.
Town-Hall, Stratford, 7, 698.
Troilus and Cressida, 38, 72, 117, 229.
True Tragedie, 9, 53.
Turnbull Street, London, 689.
Two Maids of Moreclacke, 32.
Two Noble Kinsmen, 64.
Twyne, Thomas, 132.
Tyler, Richard, 135, 256.
Underdoune, Thomas, 179.
Underhill, Hercules, 140.
Uxbridge, 463, 524, 710.
Valegio, Fr., 763.
Vander Gucht, 334, 418.

Van Dyck, Anthony, 316.
Vaughan, Robert, 365, 383.
Vavasour, Nicholas, 180.
Verginia, comedia, 90.
Vernor & Hood, 641.
Vertue, George, 386.
Visscher, J. C., 162.
Waddesdon, 475.
Wake, Isaac, 113.
Waking-Man's Dreame, 187.
Walford, E., 275.
Walton, W. L., 570.
Ward, F. & E., 547, 551, 770.
Ward, F. & G., 733.
Ward, J., 263, 686, 694, 698, 700, 762, 790, 801.
Ward, John, 42.
Ward, William, 389.
Warkmore Bridge, 704.
Warner, William, 177.
Warton, Thomas, 202.
Warwick, 312, 363, 375, 461, 475, 579.
Warwickshire, 301, 309, 312, 326, 350, 351, 618.
Water-side, 693.
Webbe, Alexander, 262.
Webster, John, 190.
Weelkes, Thomas, 209.
Welcombe Hills, 410.
Weldon, John, 56.
Welford, 673, 691, 692, 710, 780.
West, R., 553.
Westminster, 338, 539, 540.
Westminster Hall, 346.
Weston-on-Avon, 587, 599, 710, 758.
West Wickham, 448.
Whateley, George, 415.
Wheatley, co. Oxon, 354, 451, 462.
Wheler, R. B., 7, 210, 257, 388, 441, 450, 733, 770, 791.
Whetstone, George, 25, 185, 201.
Whitehall, 509.
White Lion Inn, Stratford-on-Avon, 111, 112, 591.
Whole Contention, 53.
Wier-Brake, 303, 488, 490.
Wilkins, W. H., 340.
Will, Shakespeare's, 114, 257, 723.
Williams, T., 733.
Willis, R., 284.
Wilmecote, 306, 319, 399, 404, 471, 642, 643, 647, 651, 706, 732, 769.
Wiltshire, 215, 299, 308.
Windsor, 52, 304, 323, 324, 330,

331, 332, 336, 339, 342, 343, 347, 373, 400, 408, 411, 417, 420, 465, 473, 483, 560.—*Herne's Oak*, 324, 332, 364, 419, 420, 425, 443, 790.
Windsor Street, 569.
Winter, Samuel, 366, 580.
Winter's Tale, 94.
Wirtemberg, Duke of, 402.
Witney, 71.
Wivell, A., 272, 384.
Wixford, 306, 349, 460, 475, 538, 725.
Woman is a Weathercock, 184.
Wood Street, Stratford-on-Avon, 499, 657.
Wren, Christopher, 347.
Yarranton, Andrew, 557.
Yorkshire Tragedy, 55.

TO BOOKSELLERS.

Being pretty widely known as a Shakespearean collector, hardly a week passes by without my having offers of articles which are illustrative, in one way or other, of either the works or the life of the great dramatist. Collecting, however, only in special directions, the large majority of these offers refer to objects that are outside my line of research ; and, in the belief that trouble will often be saved on both sides by an indication of the nature of that limit, I would venture to submit the following memoranda :—

I do *not* want offers of the following articles :—

Articles that are not Wanted.

1. Printed books or tracts of any description whatever that were printed either before the year 1564 or after the year 1660.
2. Painted portraits either of Shakespeare or of any member of his family.
3. Mulberry-tree or Herne's Oak relics.
4. Shakespearean engravings that have been *published* after the year 1660.

But I should feel particularly obliged by offers of the following articles :—

Articles that are Wanted.

1. Editions of Shakespeare, and books mentioning Shakespeare, that were printed before the year 1660.
2. Popular English literature, especially plays, story-books, and poems, printed during the Shakespearean period, 1564 to 1616. With the exception of

ARTICLES THAT ARE WANTED (*continued*).

editions of the plays or poems of Shakespeare which were published before the year 1660, I do not care for any books or tracts that were printed either before 1564 or after 1616.

3. Views or plans of London that were issued before the great fire of 1666, especially any which include the Southwark theatres.

4. Original sketches of objects at Stratford-on-Avon and its neighbourhood, as well as old deeds and MSS. relating to those localities.

5. Any MSS. on Shakespearean subjects by the late Edmond Malone, who died in 1812.

6. Manuscript plays written before the year 1660.

7. Autograph letters or MSS., written before the year 1840, which refer in any way to the *life* (not the works) of Shakespeare.

The London auctions are well looked after by myself for everything of the kind, but I very rarely see a country sale-catalogue, and should you be able to make me an offer of anything that comes under one or more of the above seven headings, it will be thankfully received, immediate payment following its acceptance.

J. O. HALLIWELL-PHILLIPPS.

Hollingbury Copse, Brighton,
July, 1887.

www.ingramcontent.com/pod-product-compliance
Lightning Source LLC
Chambersburg PA
CBHW030242170426
43202CB00009B/594